CAMBRIDGE STUDIES IN LINGUISTICS

General Editors: W.SIDNEY ALLEN, B.COMRIE, C.J.FILLMORE
E.J.A.HENDERSON, F.W.HOUSEHOLDER, R.LASS, J.LYONS
P.H.MATTHEWS, R.B.LE PAGE, F.R.PALMER, R.POSNER
J.L.M.TRIM

Variation in an English dialect
A sociolinguistic study

In this series

1 DAVID CRYSTAL: *Prosodic systems and intonation in English**

3 RODNEY D. HUDDLESTON: *The sentence in written English*

4 JOHN M. ANDERSON: *The grammar of case**

5 M. L. SAMUELS: *Linguistic evolution**

6 P. H. MATTHEWS: *Inflectional morphology**

7 GILLIAN BROWN: *Phonological rules and dialect variation**

8 BRIAN NEWTON: *The generative interpretation of dialect**

9 R. M. W. DIXON: *The Dyirbal language of North Queensland**

10 BRUCE L. DERWING: *Transformational grammar as a theory of language acquisition**

11 MELISSA BOWERMAN: *Early syntactic development**

12 W. SIDNEY ALLEN: *Accent and rhythm*

13 PETER TRUDGILL: *The social differentiation of English in Norwich**

14 ROGER LASS and JOHN M. ANDERSON: *Old English phonology*

15 RUTH M. KEMPSON: *Presupposition and the delimitation of semantics**

16 JAMES R. HURFORD: *The linguistic theory of numerals*

17 ROGER LASS: *English phonology and phonological theory*

18 G. M. AWBERY: *The syntax of Welsh*

19 R. M. W. DIXON: *A grammar of Yidiɲ*

20 JAMES FOLEY: *Foundations of theoretical phonology*

21 A. RADFORD: *Italian syntax: transformational and relational grammar*

22 DIETER WUNDERLICH: *Foundations of linguistics**

23 DAVID W. LIGHTFOOT: *Principles of diachronic syntax**

24 ANNETTE KARMILOFF-SMITH: *A functional approach to child language**

25 PER LINELL: *Psychological reality in phonology*

26 CHRISTINE TANZ: *Studies in the acquisition of deictic terms*

27 ROGER LASS: *On explaining language change*

28 TORBEN THRANE: *Referential–semantic analysis*

29 TAMSIN DONALDSON: *Ngiyambaa*

30 KRISTJÁN ÁRNASON: *Quantity in historical phonology*

31 JOHN LAVER: *The phonetic description of voice quality*

32 PETER AUSTIN: *A grammar of Diyari, South Australia*

33 ALICE C. HARRIS: *Georgian syntax*

34 SUZANNE ROMAINE: *Socio-historical linguistics*

35 MARTIN ATKINSON: *Explanations in the study of child language development*

36 SUZANNE FLEISCHMAN: *The future in thought and language*

37 JENNY CHESHIRE: *Variation in an English dialect*

* *Issued in hard covers and as a paperback*

VARIATION IN
AN ENGLISH DIALECT

A sociolinguistic study

JENNY CHESHIRE

Lecturer in Linguistics
University of Bath

CAMBRIDGE UNIVERSITY PRESS

CAMBRIDGE
LONDON   NEW YORK   NEW ROCHELLE
MELBOURNE   SYDNEY

Published by the Press Syndicate of the University of Cambridge
The Pitt Building, Trumpington Street, Cambridge CB2 1RP
32 East 57th Street, New York, NY 10022, USA
296 Beaconsfield Parade, Middle Park, Melbourne 3206, Australia

First published 1982

Printed in Great Britain at the University Press, Cambridge

Library of Congress catalogue card number: 82–4189

British Library Cataloguing in Publication Data
Cheshire, Jenny
Variation in an English dialect. – (Cambridge
studies in linguistics, ISSN 0068–676X; 37)
1. English language – Dialects   2. English
language – Social aspects
I. Title
306.4 (expanded)   PE1711
ISBN 0 521 23802 1

Contents

Acknowledgements   ix
Introduction   1

PART I: METHODOLOGY

1 Preliminary considerations   **5**
1.1 Nonlinguistic variation   5
1.2 The vernacular   5
1.3 Speech style   6
1.4 The Observer's Paradox   7
1.5 Adolescents as a source of data   8
1.6 The elderly as a source of data   11
1.7 Vernacular culture   12

2 Data collection   **13**
2.1 The adventure playgrounds   13
2.2 Recording procedures   14
2.3 The data   15
2.4 The speakers   21
   2.4.1 Ages of speakers   22
   2.4.2 Linguistic backgrounds of speakers   23
   2.4.3 Occupations of parents   24

3 Methods of analysis   **26**

PART II: LINGUISTIC VARIATION

4 Verb forms   **31**
4.1 Present tense verb forms   31
   4.1.1 Present tense forms of HAVE   32
   4.1.2 Linguistic change and HAVE   33
   4.1.3 Present tense forms of DO   34
   4.1.4 Linguistic change and DO   36
   4.1.5 Linguistic constraints on regular present tense verb forms   39
   4.1.6 The following complement constraint   39
   4.1.7 The 'vernacular verb' constraint   42
4.2 Past tense verb forms   44
   4.2.1 Past tense forms of BE   44

4.2.2 Other past tense forms   46
4.3 Tense in conditional sentences   49

5 Negation   51
5.1 *Ain't*   51
   5.1.1 Standard English forms   52
   5.1.2 Linguistic constraints on *ain't*   52
   5.1.3 Derivation of *ain't*   53
   5.1.4 Phonetic realisations of *ain't*   54
   5.1.5 Semantic functions of tag questions   57
   5.1.6 Continuing linguistic change in the form of *ain't*   61
5.2 Negative concord   63
   5.2.1 Negative concord in Reading English   63
5.3 *Never*   67
   5.3.1 *Never* as a negative preterite   67
   5.3.2 Linguistic constraints on *never*   69
   5.3.3 Syntactic status of *never*   70

6 Relative pronouns   72
6.1 Forms of the relative pronoun   72
6.2 Comparison with standard English forms   73
6.3 Linguistic constraints on forms of the pronoun   74

7 Other nonstandard forms   76
7.1 Prepositions   76
7.2 Demonstratives   78
7.3 Reflexive pronouns   79
7.4 Nouns of measurement   79
7.5 Adverbial constructions   80
   7.5.1 Comparative adverbs   80
   7.5.2 Non-distinction of adverbial and adjectival forms   80
7.6 'Intrusive' -*s*   81

PART III: SOCIOLINGUISTIC VARIATION

8 Social variation   85
8.1 Sociolinguistic analyses   85
8.2 Variation with sex of speaker   85
8.3 Variation with peer group status   87
8.4 The 'vernacular' and 'legitimate' sub-cultures   94
   8.4.1 The vernacular culture index   97
   8.4.2 Linguistic markers of adherence to the vernacular culture   102
8.5 Vernacular culture and its effect on girls   106

9 Stylistic variation   112
9.1 Constraints on speech style   112
9.2 The school recordings   113
9.3 Variation in speech style   114

Conclusion   127
Appendix   132
Bibliography   134
Index of authors   138
General index   140

TO PAUL

Acknowledgements

This study is based on research which I carried out at the University of Reading for my Ph.D. dissertation, and which was supported by grants from the S.S.R.C. and from the University of Reading. I would particularly like to thank my supervisor, Peter Trudgill, whose work stimulated this research and who provided constant encouragement, patience and good advice throughout the entire period. I would also like to thank Frank Palmer for his sound advice and constructive criticisms, not only during the initial research period but also during the reworking and rewriting that has resulted in this book. I am also grateful to Viv Edwards for her helpful comments on the manuscript, and to Jean Aitchison for her insights into some of the implications that the research findings have for language change. Thanks are also due to Jane Maxim for the use of her recordings of elderly speakers and to Ron Winter for help with the diagrams. None of these people, of course, can be held responsible for the shortcomings of the book.

I am grateful to the head-teachers and teachers at the following schools for their co-operation with the school recordings: Ridgeway Primary School, Alfred Sutton Boys' School, Southlands Girls' School, Cintra Secondary School and Highdown School.

Special thanks go to Paul Cheshire for his extreme forbearance, moral support and practical help throughout, and to my children Jack and Sally Cheshire for maintaining their customary ebullience and lively disregard for scholarly enterprise.

I am grateful also to Margaret Lambden and Pat Richardson for their excellent typing, and to Barry Abbott and Barbara Abbott for coming to the rescue at a critical moment.

My final thanks are due to the children who provided the data for this research (their names have been changed in this book), and with whom I spent many lively and enjoyable hours in the adventure playgrounds. They would doubtless be most surprised at the result!

Frontispiece   Oil painting, 'Newtown Adventure Playground',
by Christopher Hall. Reproduced by kind permission of the artist

Introduction

The work described here was motivated by the belief that variation is an inherent characteristic of natural language, and that a full understanding of language must include an understanding of the nature and the function of variation. The aim of the book is to analyse some of the linguistic and sociolinguistic variation that occurs in natural, spontaneous, everyday speech. This means that its chief contribution is, perhaps, to the study of language in its social context; but the results of the analysis have theoretical implications for both synchronic and diachronic linguistics.

Any variety of English (or, indeed, of any language) could provide data for the analysis of variation; the nonstandard regional and social varieties, however, are particularly suitable for this kind of study, since most nonstandard linguistic features occur variably in contemporary English, alternating in occurrence with the corresponding standard English forms. The analysis in this study, therefore, will be based on natural conversational interaction between speakers of a nonstandard variety of English – the variety spoken in the town of Reading, in Berkshire.

The relationship that exists between the socioeconomic status of speakers and their use of nonstandard variable forms has been well documented, and no attempt will be made to replicate these findings here. Instead, the analysis focuses on speakers of a single socioeconomic class (the 'working class'), in an attempt to gain some insight into the more subtle aspects of variation.

Most previous studies have dealt with phonological variation, and there are many practical advantages in this. But if we are to further our understanding of language, it is necessary to extend the analysis of variation beyond this level, and for this reason the study will be concerned with morphological and syntactic variation. This means that it will also provide a valid description of the morphological and syntactic differences between standard English and a variety of English used by working-class speakers – a description which is long overdue. Speculative theories about the differences between the language of working-class speakers and that of middle-class speakers have been given credence in educational circles, but these theories have rarely been based on an empirical analysis of real language. Rosen (1972: 14), for example, makes the following point: 'It cannot be repeated too often that, for all Bernstein's work, we know little about working-class language.'

By focusing on a nonstandard variety of English, the study will also make a contribution to the field of dialectology.

Part I of the book discusses the methodology that is involved in making observations of natural everyday interaction. It outlines the fieldwork procedures that were used in this study, and describes some of the social characteristics of the speakers, as well as the adventure playgrounds where most of the data were collected. The main linguistic analysis is given in Part II. Linguistic variation is analysed from two interacting points of view: the extent to which speakers fluctuate between the non-standard form of a variable and the corresponding standard English form; and the extent to which their fluctuation is affected by the immediate linguistic environment of the variable. Where relevant, the relationship between variation and language change will be explored. Part III analyses sociolinguistic variation, again from two interacting points of view. First, the ways in which different groups of speakers use the nonstandard forms are analysed, in order to establish the social significance of the different linguistic variables; next, the ways in which individual speakers use the nonstandard forms are investigated, in an attempt to understand the ways in which speakers are able to exploit the resources of the language system to convey social meaning. Finally, the main theoretical implications of the study are discussed in the Conclusion.

PART I: METHODOLOGY

1 *Preliminary considerations*

1.1 Nonlinguistic variation

Variation in language is an extremely complex phenomenon, and it
would be quite unrealistic to attempt to analyse all aspects of it. It is
possible, however, to devise a methodology which will eliminate those
aspects of variation that are already well understood, and which will
allow us to focus on some of the less obvious factors.

It is well known, for example, that variation at all levels of language can
be correlated with certain nonlinguistic features, such as the age, sex and
socioeconomic class of speakers (see, for example, Trudgill, 1974); the
nature of the relationship between speakers and the extent to which they
share a mutual goal (Giles and St Clair, 1979); and the topic, channel and
setting of the speech event (Hymes, 1967). It makes sense, therefore, to
attempt to eliminate from the analysis as many as possible of these
nonlinguistic constraints on variation. The fieldwork procedures used
here aimed to record groups of speakers who were of roughly the same
age and who were from similar social backgrounds; the groups were
single-sex peer groups, who shared a number of common values and
activities. The recordings always took place in the same setting (adventure playgrounds in the town), and although the topics of conversation
could obviously not be controlled there were, in fact, many recurrent
themes in the conversations. A few of the better-known aspects of
sociolinguistic variation, therefore, were eliminated from the study.

1.2 The vernacular

As noted in the Introduction, this analysis is based on the nonstandard
variety of English spoken in the town of Reading; and it will focus on the
speech of a single socioeconomic group. The relationship between social
and regional variation in Britain is well known; it is often represented by a

triangle, as in Figure 1, with speakers from the upper socioeconomic classes using predominantly standard English features, and speakers from the lower socioeconomic classes using more nonstandard regional features. The 'purest' varieties will be heard from speakers at either end of the social scale, who have traditionally been more socially isolated; although the intervening classes may show considerably greater variation in their speech, the patterns of variation may be inconsistent and unsystematic (see Labov, 1972b: 134). Since this study aims to discover patterns of linguistic variation in nonstandard English, it makes sense to choose speakers from the lower end of the socioeconomic scale, who will use nonstandard linguistic forms most consistently. This variety of speech is both popularly and more technically known as 'the vernacular'.

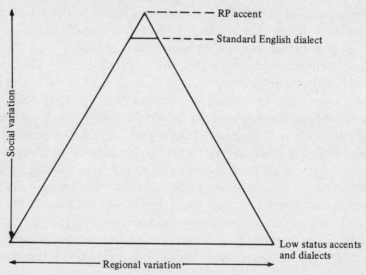

Figure 1   (from Trudgill, 1975: 21)

1.3 Speech style

The term 'vernacular' is sometimes used with a second sense, which has to do with the effect of speech style on linguistic variation. The Labovian framework of analysis sees speech style as forming a linear continuum, which reflects the amount of attention that speakers give to their speech. It is assumed that in formal situations they will monitor their linguistic behaviour, perhaps unconsciously; and that they will, as a result, tend to use a higher proportion of the socially prestigious standard English forms. In informal situations, where speakers are more relaxed, less attention will be given to speech, and a more natural and spontaneous style will be used. It is the style at the extreme informal end of the stylistic continuum that is known as 'vernacular'. Thus all speakers have a vernacular style, but the frequency of nonstandard forms that they use in this style varies, depending, as we have seen, on their socioeconomic class.

Labov maintains that it is in the vernacular speech style that the most consistent patterns of variation are to be observed (1972c: 112). It will be suggested later in this study that the Labovian linear concept of style is over-simplistic. It seems true, though, that when speakers are relaxed they will use their most natural speech style, and that it is in this style that variation will be at its most consistent level.

It follows, then, that our analysis of linguistic variation in spontaneous natural speech should be based on the most informal style of working-class speakers – on the vernacular style of 'the vernacular'.

1.4 The Observer's Paradox

The problem of the Observer's Paradox is well known: studies of language in its social context aim to discover how people talk in everyday life, rather than how they talk when they are being tape recorded by a linguist; but unfortunately linguists cannot analyse everyday language without making tape recordings first.

Early studies of language in its social context used tape recorded interviews as data, and extracted from the interview isolated stretches of informal speech. The problem here, though, as these studies freely admit, is that an interview is inevitably a formal situation, so that however friendly and relaxed speakers may appear to be, it must always be assumed that they have a still more casual speech style that they use when they are not being recorded – when they are at home, for example, with their family and friends.

Recent surveys have attempted to develop a methodology that will overcome, or at least alleviate, the problem of the Observer's Paradox: for example, by working as 'a friend of a friend' within social networks (see Milroy, 1980), or by asking speakers to make recordings themselves, so that the linguist need not be present (see Wilson, forthcoming). However, the analysis of morphological and syntactic variation imposes some specific constraints on the fieldwork techniques. The main problem is that very large quantities of data are necessary in order to ensure an adequate number of occurrences of the variables; and if linguistic constraints on variation are to be successfully isolated, these occurrences need to be in a wide range of different linguistic environments. Speakers have to be persuaded, therefore, to co-operate in the collection of large quantities of data. Furthermore, it may not become apparent that more data are required until the analysis is already under way, which means that the investigator will have to go back to the informants to make further recordings. This will only be possible if the fieldworker has had time to build up a good relationship with speakers.

One method that allows for these eventualities is 'long-term participant-observation', where the fieldworker gets to know a pre-existing group of speakers, and becomes semi-incorporated into the group for a period of time. The method rests on the assumption that the social pressures exerted by group norms of behaviour will ensure that the natural interaction of the group continues, despite the presence of an outside, or semi-outside, observer.

The most successful use of this method was in Labov et al.'s New York study (1968), where a club-house in Harlem was rented for a year, and adolescent groups from the area taken in a 'bugged' minibus for recording sessions at the university. Lack of funds and personnel may prevent these methods from being directly copied elsewhere, but it seems that they can be adapted without jeopardising too severely the recording of natural spontaneous speech.

1.5 Adolescents as a source of data

One reason given by Labov for choosing to analyse the speech of adolescents in his Harlem study is that patterns of variation are likely to be more consistent in the speech of adolescents than in the speech of older subjects. Labov (1965) sets out a model for the acquisition of standard English, which shows the peer group as exerting an increasing influence on speakers between the ages of 5 to 12, at which point it becomes the major influence on speech. His subjective evaluation tests confirm that it is not until the age of about 14 that children in New York City show an awareness of the social significance of different varieties of language. He concludes, therefore, that the speech of adolescents is less subject to style-shifting, and that there is a greater likelihood of obtaining recordings of pure vernacular speech if adolescents are used as the source of data.

Other studies, however, do not support Labov's model. In Edinburgh, for example, regular patterns of stylistic variation were observed in children as young as 10, which suggests that in this variety of British English, at least, children are aware of the social significance of linguistic variables at a relatively early age (see Romaine, 1975; Reid, 1978). The available evidence is conflicting, for in Glasgow regular patterns of stylistic variation were not found until speakers had reached the age of 15 (Macaulay, 1977). As far as varieties of British English are concerned, then, it seems that there are considerable differences in the ages at which style-shifting is acquired, so it does not necessarily follow that using adolescents as subjects will lead to recordings of pure vernacular speech.

There are, however, several other advantages in using adolescents as subjects, particularly where the method of long-term participant-observation is used. As we have seen, this method depends upon recording members of a pre-existing group, in order that group pressures may overcome the potentially inhibiting effect of an outside observer. An initial stage in the fieldwork procedures, therefore, involves identifying speakers who belong to a cohesive peer group. In the case of adolescents such speakers are extremely easy to identify, for the norms that govern their speech also govern other kinds of behaviour, including the way they dress. The style of dress that peer group members adopt generally depends on the fashions of the moment, and it is reasonable to assume that adolescents who do not conform to the current style are less susceptible to peer group pressures and less suitable, therefore, as subjects for linguistic fieldwork.

A further advantage lies in the fact that once adolescent peer group members have been identified, it is relatively easy to make contact with them. In Britain adolescent peer groups often congregate in certain fixed places on the streets; this means that they can be approached on neutral territory, where neither the fieldworker nor the adolescents have a clearly defined social role (as they would have, for example, in their houses or schools). It also means that the fieldworker can make spontaneous (or apparently spontaneous) visits to the meeting places, which will lead to a more friendly and relaxed situation than would be possible if a precise time for a visit had to be arranged.

Where large quantities of data are required, as was the case, for example, in the present study, speakers have to be prepared to give up a great deal of time to the fieldworker. This often causes problems where adult speakers are concerned, particularly when they lead busy lives.

Adolescents, however, are one of the few groups in society who have plenty of time to spare, and this is particularly true during school holidays (if they play truant from school, of course, they have still more time to spare). Many adolescents confess to being bored, so they are pleased to meet new people and willing to spend time with them.

Perhaps the strongest advantage of working with adolescents is that it is relatively easy for an outsider to become accepted by the group. To some extent this may be because they are young enough to retain some of the child's unquestioning acceptance of adult behaviour, so that where adults might be hesitant about being recorded, adolescents will accept it as an activity in its own right. They are also more likely to be familiar with recording equipment and less inhibited, as a result, by its presence. All the speakers who took part in this study had their own cassette recorders, and they were all used to working with tape recorders at school. Fieldworkers are, of course, more likely to be accepted by a group if they adapt to some of the group norms. Dress, for example, has a great deal of social significance, and whilst it would be ludicrous for fieldworkers temporarily to adopt teenage fashions, it is not difficult to dress informally, in a style that is acceptable to the adolescent age group. Furthermore, adolescents who conform to peer group values often reject many of the values held by mainstream society, so if fieldworkers behave in any way that deviates slightly from conventional norms they are more likely to be accepted. Different fieldworkers will have their own eccentricities; for the present study, behaviour that may have helped towards acceptance by the group was the use of a motorbike to travel to and from the meeting places (which, incidentally, served as a useful initial topic of conversation).

There are, however, at least two serious drawbacks to a study that is confined to adolescent speakers. Firstly, the resulting analysis will pertain only to the language of a small and relatively isolated group in society; it may, therefore, present a limited or even distorted view of language. A solution is to supplement the main data collection with what Labov has termed 'unsystematic observation'. In the present study, for example, I listened to adult conversations in shops, launderettes, street markets and public houses and on public transport, in order to check that the linguistic features heard in the speech of the adolescent groups also occurred in the speech of adults.

Secondly, a study that is limited to a single age group is unable to do more than speculate on the role of language change in variation, which means that the analysis of variation will lack explanatory power. Recent research, for example, has investigated language change by making studies in 'apparent time': by comparing, that is to say, the language of speakers who belong to different generations but who otherwise have the same regional and social characteristics. It does not necessarily follow, of course, that any differences in their speech will be due to language change, and particular caution is required where the language of adolescents is concerned, since this may include temporary specialised features (for discussion, see Chambers and Trudgill, 1980: 165–6). But the technique can be useful as a way of cautiously confirming indications that variation is the result of language change.

Another way of investigating the role of language change is by consulting earlier dialect records and contrasting current usage with earlier usage. Unfortunately, however, fieldwork procedures used in early dialect work are often unsatisfactory by current standards, so that while dialect records may give some idea of forms that were used at the time, they certainly cannot constitute reliable evidence. The only records that are available for comparison with the findings of the present study, for example, are those of the *Survey of English Dialects* (Orton and Dieth, 1962–71). Any such comparison, however, would be quite invalid, since the *S.E.D.* is not based on informal conversational interaction; nor does it cover the urban variety of English spoken in the town of Reading.

1.6 The elderly as a source of data

Curiously enough, many of the advantages of using adolescents as linguistic subjects also apply to the elderly. Like adolescents, the elderly are somewhat isolated nowadays from the rest of society; this means that they may be bored or lonely and prepared, as a result, to spend time in conversations with a fieldworker.

In an attempt to compensate for the lack of evidence concerning language change that results from the use of a single age group, this study will make occasional reference to part of a pre-existing collection of data that was compiled for a separate research project (Maxim, forthcoming). The data consist of a series of tape recorded interviews between a female fieldworker and a number of working-class men and women aged 70 or over, who had lived all their lives in Reading. Clearly no systematic comparison is possible between these more formalised interviews and the informal conversational data obtained from the adolescents, and none will be attempted; but these interviews will occasionally be used as a way of investigating linguistic change in 'apparent time'.

1.7 Vernacular culture

The traditional Labovian view of the speech community is that its members share a common set of evaluative overt norms that assigns prestige to standard English forms, whilst an opposing set of covert norms controls the street culture and is responsible for the consistent vernacular of the urban working class (Labov, 1973b: 83). There is evidence from a number of empirical studies that norms of this kind do exist (see, for example, Trudgill, 1972; Labov et al., 1968; and Part III of this book). Again, however, difficulties have sometimes been experienced in applying these concepts to varieties of British English (see Romaine, 1980: 193–4).

The overt norms are maintained and transmitted by the established institutions in society, including, of course, the school, whilst the covert norms of the vernacular culture are transmitted by the peer group. This study, as we have seen, aims to analyse consistent vernacular speech, and it is essential, therefore, that speakers should belong to a peer group whose behaviour is governed by vernacular norms, rather than by the norms of the school. (That the two sets of norms may be considered mutually exclusive will be seen when the nature of vernacular norms is considered in Part III.)

2 Data collection

2.1 The adventure playgrounds

We have established so far that the analysis should be based on the speech of working-class adolescent peer groups, whose behaviour should conform more closely to the values of the street culture than to those of the mainstream culture in society. As we have seen, the school is one of the main agents of mainstream culture; ideal subjects, therefore, would be relatively uninvolved in school life. Thus a useful way of locating suitable peer groups for the study was to look in working-class areas of the town of Reading during school hours, when members of the street culture might be playing truant from school.

This led to the discovery of an adventure playground which was the regular meeting place for a group of boys who lived in the area. The playground was in Orts Road, in an area of Reading known as Newtown. This is an Educational Priority area (see Plowden Report, 1967: 57–9) to the east of the town centre. Orts Road runs alongside the Kennet and Avon Canal, and is opposite a biscuit factory and the town gasworks. The houses in which the boys lived have now been demolished; they were late-nineteenth-century houses backing onto the canal, and were damp, in poor repair and, according to the boys, overrun by rats. The playground itself was on a small derelict patch of waste ground at the end of the road, next to a public house. It contained an abandoned, rusting car, some empty oil cans (used as drums by the boys) and a ramshackle wooden structure which the boys had built but which they later burnt down. The playground was subsidised by the Berkshire County Council (though the funds that it received were minimal), and a semi-voluntary 'playleader' was sometimes there during school holidays (it was the playleader who had organised the boys into building the wooden climbing frame).

When the playground was first discovered there were two boys outside, taunting passers-by. They were asked if they could be visited the next day, and whether they would bring some of their friends along. At the time it seemed that a reason for the visit should be offered, though in retrospect this was unnecessary. It was essential, however, if natural spontaneous speech was to be obtained, for the boys not to know that their language was the object of study. I told them, therefore, that I was a university student and that I had a vacation job helping in research to find out what people in Reading thought of the town. The use of a tape recorder was explained as necessary because I had a bad memory and could not remember what people told me. The story made my role as observer a neutral one, since it seemed that I was simply doing a job, and had no personal interest in the tape recordings. It also meant that there was some fellow-feeling between us: I was apparently told what to do by some person of higher authority, I needed some money (hence the vacation job), and I apparently did not do too well at the job, since I needed a tape recorder to help me. In fact, however, the reason for my visits was never mentioned after the first two occasions.

The Orts Road boys told me where a second adventure playground could be found. This was at Shinfield, an area to the south of Reading containing a mixture of housing, including large detached upper-income houses and some middle-income new development. The playground was immediately behind a Council housing estate built in the 1930s, which was used to rehouse several families from areas that were to be demolished, such as Orts Road. This playground was larger and better organised, and used by more children; the playleader took the children swimming twice a week, by minibus, organised jumble sales to raise funds, and brought paints and clay for the children to use. A large wooden climbing frame had been built, as at Orts Road, and there was also a home-made wooden space rocket (which was later burnt down) and two semi-underground rooms with corrugated iron roofs. Both this playground and the Orts Road playground were unpopular with local residents, mainly because of the fires and fights that took place there, and some of the local children had been forbidden to go there by their parents.

This time no fabricated story was used: I simply began chatting to a small group of girls, and asked if I could come back the next day with a tape recorder. They were mildly curious but accepted quite readily.

2.2 Recording procedures

Both playgrounds were visited two or three times a week for a period of nine months, during which time a very friendly relationship was established between the children and myself. Various techniques were used to produce a suitably relaxed atmosphere for the recordings. For example, we usually chewed gum and ate sweets during the visits (admittedly this sometimes made it difficult to hear the precise phonological forms of variables), and the boys always smoked. No attempts were made to organise speakers into groups: usually two or three children would come up to chat when I arrived, and later others would join the group, whereupon the first few might wander off. At least three speakers were present during each recording, and usually there were more than three. Topics of conversation were left to occur spontaneously, and the children were left to interact without interruption. Most of the recordings were made sitting on the grass in the playgrounds; a few were made on the climbing frames and in the underground rooms at Shinfield, but these were of poor technical quality since the microphone was shaken by people running and jumping nearby.

For the majority of the recordings a Uher two-track stereophonic recorder was used. Two microphones were set on the ground, at opposite angles so as to receive input from all speakers. This produced recordings of very good quality; the only interference was caused by aeroplanes (particularly Concorde) and by the children's radios. There was little passing traffic, as the playgrounds were in quiet residential areas.

When the playground recordings had all been completed, the schools that the children attended were contacted. Their teachers were asked to make a recording of the speakers with two or three of their friends. I did not take part in these recordings; nevertheless, contact with the schools had to wait until this later stage, as the friendly relationship that existed at the playgrounds would have been severely jeopardised had the children thought that I was connected with their schools. Not all the teachers were willing to co-operate, but a limited set of data of a more formal speech style was obtained, which will be of some analytical interest.

2.3 The data

Many of the recorded conversations were extremely lively and noisy; others, particularly where fewer speakers were involved, were quieter. The livelier conversations contained a great many jokes, wisecracks and witticisms; the following extract provides an example, and illustrates a typical rapid joke sequence:

Ed:	Got a light?
Derek:	Here, I'm looking down the lady's bag – silly old bag!
Ed:	Here, cop hold of that for a bit, I'll go and get a light off Al.
Nobby:	I'll go and get a light, I've got a fag.
Ed:	I'll go. I'll go and get his lighter.
Jeff:	(to passing girls) Maiow, maiow, maiow.
Nobby:	Here, I've got one – Doctor, doctor, I got diarrhoea. When did you first know? When I took the bicycle clips off. Doctor, doctor, I keep thinking I'm a pair of curtains. Go on, man, pull yourself together.
Jeff:	Doctor, doctor, I think I'm a dog. When did the trouble start? When I was a puppy.
Benny:	No, no – Doctor, doctor, I keep thinking I'm a dog. You'd better lay on the couch, tell me all about it. Sorry, I'm not allowed on the couch. Why did the bloke take a ladder to bed?
Derek:	To get up in the morning.
Benny:	(to passer-by) Wotcher, missis. Get 'em off!
Jeff:	See if I knows you. (whistles)
Benny:	Drop them! See if I know you.
Jenny:	Who's that?
Benny:	Don't know. That's why I say get them off, see if I knows you. Don't blush, missis!
Jeff:	Down, Benny, now, Benny, stop it, Benny!

The recordings also contain a large number of narrative accounts. These were enjoyed by all the participants; when speakers were about to launch into a narrative their friends often called other members of the peer group over to listen, and good story-tellers enjoyed great prestige within the peer group. A good example of a narrative account is given below (although it should be borne in mind that a great deal of the 'performance value' is lost in a written transcript):

Ed:	I see that Clockwork Orange film twenty-seven – no, twenty-six times, I see that.
Jenny:	Oh God, did you? I thought that was a horrible film.
Ed:	Bloody beautiful, mate.
Benny:	What happened then, Ed? Go on, tell us all about it.
Ed:	Do you want me to tell you all about it?
Benny:	Yeah.
Nobby:	Yeah.
Ed:	Right. Well here y'are, mate, they're in this caff, right, and there's all nude women, right.

Benny:	Yeah (laughs).
Ed:	No, no, it's milk they have. I don't know, it builds you up, like drugs it is and that, right. Right?
Jeff:	Have you seen it?
Jenny:	Yeah.
Ed:	And they go out –
Derek:	He's telling a story, come on (calls to other boys).
Ed:	They go out, and they get in this, like a, sea buggy, isn't it, did you see it, did you?
Jenny:	Yeah.
Ed:	Like a beach buggy, isn't it?
Jenny:	Can't remember.
Ed:	I'm sure it was a beach buggy, and they go out. Go all down this country lane, mate, and there's all lorries coming, but they don't move over, just straight down the middle of the road – don't they? – motorbikes go flying over the edge. Arrive at this house, see, put the old mask on, get in there. Have a good time with the old missis, kick hell out of the old man, puts the ball in his mouth, 'singing in the rain' (sings), boot, kick him in the head about twenty times, you know. Anyway, then she dies. And then, going on in the film a bit they meet the Hell's Angels, don't they?
Jenny:	That's right. And they have a big fight with them, don't they?
Ed:	Hold it, yeah, but – them Hell's Angels were having this piece, see, ripping all her clothes off, mate, on this stage, just getting on her, like that. And the old skinheads come, mate, the old boys, Billyboy, the skinhead went round, you gypsy. Got the old flick-knife, have we? He did, honest, that's what he goes. Got the old flick-knife out? And all these boys, just stood there, and all these greebos, there was about six of them, or five of them, just come out, there was four of them, you know, standing there. And the old chains come out, the old iron bar, mate, boom, all these greebos just flying out the place, they were. That's all I can remember.

Other narratives occurred during the course of conversations, as below:

Jenny:	Yes, but – I bet your mum and dad don't swear though, do they?
Derek:	My dad do, mate. Especially when he's in the car. If anybody goes in front of him, he goes 'oo er er'. (laughter)
Rob:	We was going along in his dad's car, right, and this bloke

was walking across the crossing, with a load of chips, and he goes, 'Fucking hurry up, you bastard, or I'll knock the chips out your hand!'
(laughter)

Derek: And there was one day, when we went to Southampton to watch the cricket, there was me, my mum and my brother, you see. Say that's the parking thing there, and we couldn't get out. So we just got out, and then, my dad wanted to turn round but the car was coming along there too close to him, so, till then we was all waiting there, holding the traffic up for about quarter of an hour, 'cos, just 'cos that other bloke wouldn't move. And then my dad was, got out and started swearing at him and everything, then my dad said, 'If you lot wasn't here, I'd have got out and smashed his head in,' or something like that. That's the only reason why he never, 'cos me and my brother was in there.

Jenny: He sounds quite rough.

Nobby: This bloke kept, he knocked my dad, he was . . . my dad was shaving a pig off, and he knocked his knife in the water tank. And this bloke started running. And my dad picked up this thing, what they shaves the pigs with and pulls their nails off, and threw it at him. And if he didn't pick up a tin and put it in front of his face, it would have hit him straight in the face.

Rob: Was he drunk, was he?

Nobby: No, the first time my mum met my dad he got drunk. So she took his wallet to see how much was in there. There was three hundred quid in there.

Rob: Bloody hell, what's your old man walking around with all that in his pocket for? What, did he bloody rob a bank?

Nobby: I don't know, he'd just been paid.

Rob: Mad.

Verbal skills were an important part of the peer group culture, and speakers were extremely talkative, so there were never any problems in eliciting speech. Normal verbal interactions did not appear to change when the groups were being recorded: swearing, obscenities and laughter continued, for example, and 'taboo' subjects were discussed at length. Physical interaction also remained unchanged, with fights and scuffles developing during recording sessions – to such an extent, in fact, that at one point the recording equipment had to be packed away for fear that it would be broken. Fighting, of course, did not help to produce recordings of good technical quality, but the fact that it took place suggests that the speech style was suitably relaxed, for speakers appeared totally to have forgotten that they were being recorded. It is possible, of course, that some of the profusive swearing and obscenities that occurred were acts of linguistic bravado, caused by the presence of the tape recorder; but generally speakers did not refer to the microphone, and although it was always in evidence, it usually seemed to have been overlooked.

Some of the recorded material could not be used because of fights or background interference, or because too many people were talking at the same time. The total data used as the basis for analysis amounted to eighteen hours of speech.

A further four hours of speech were obtained from the school recordings made by teachers. A minimum of three friends took part in these recordings, so the main differences between these and the recordings made at the playground were the fact that they took place in school and the fact that the teacher was present. The teachers had mainly chosen topics of conversation that were of interest to the children, such as motorbikes and discos. The precise linguistic differences between the school recordings and the playground recordings will be discussed in Part III. The most striking general difference, however, was that the school recordings were more restrained, with very few jokes and wisecracks. Some conversations had an 'interview' structure, with questions asked by the teacher and relatively short answers given by the children. These provided only minimal quantities of data, as can be seen from the following example:

Teacher:	Right. Now I want you to tell me, Ann, what your class-room looks like.
	(silence)
Teacher:	What sort of things do you have on the walls?
Ann:	Pictures, paintings, my dolls.
Teacher:	What else?
Ann:	Um.
Teacher:	Do you have any pets in your room, Jason?
Jason:	Yes, we got two hamsters, guinea pigs like, and one goldfish and two turtles.
Teacher:	Anything else?
Jason:	No.
Teacher:	No. That's a lot to look after. Who looks after them?
Darren:	Um. John.
Teacher:	Do you all look after them or have you got special people who look –
Darren:	Yes.
Teacher:	Special people?

Darren:	Yes.
Teacher:	Right. What sort of games do you play in the playtime, Ann?
Ann:	I play skipping.
Teacher:	Skipping . . .
Ann:	With my friends.
Teacher:	Mmm. What else?
	(silence)

Other conversations bore more resemblance to the playground recordings, containing narrative accounts and little interruption from the teacher, as in this example:

Teacher:	Do you both go rabbiting?
Tommy:	Yeah, lots of us do.
Dave:	I goes rabbiting over Twyford Bridge.
Teacher:	How do you go about it? I mean, how do you do your rabbiting?
Dave:	Well, there's a burrow, isn't there?
Tommy:	Yeah, and then you put the nets over the hole, get –
Dave:	Get a ferret.
Tommy:	– get a ferret, and you put the ferret down the hole, and if there's a rabbit in there it'll come out. And you all stand back, away from the holes. So the rabbits can't see us as they come out. As they come out they hits the net and the net folds up with it between them. Goes through the net.
Dave:	Just grab hold of them and break their neck.
Teacher:	Oh I see, so it sort of runs into the net.
Dave:	Runs into the net, yeah.
Tommy:	There's two clips –
Dave:	Yeah. There's a net, and it's got this cord and a peg on it, and the peg, kind of, you put the peg –
Tommy:	– put the peg in the ground –
Dave:	– in the ground, and it's got this cord round it.
Tommy:	Yeah, the net's in the middle.
Dave:	And once the rabbit goes in the net, the peg's in the ground, and it –
Tommy:	– pulls –
Dave:	– it pulls the net up tight.
Tommy:	So it can't get out. It tries to get out, and it breaks its neck.

Conversations of this kind formed the main body of data for the analysis of the 'school style' of speech.

2.4 The speakers

We saw earlier that an essential requirement for this study was that speakers should have similar social characteristics. The fieldwork procedures used here, however, meant that the sociological variables could not be systematically controlled, since speakers were not pre-selected, but were members of naturally occurring peer groups. Clearly speakers could not be asked for detailed personal information about their parents' incomes or levels of education without jeopardising the informal, friendly relationships of the playground; yet I needed to obtain some kind of sociological information in order to check that speakers met the requirements of the study.

The concept of social class is, of course, a very complex one, and it has been defined in a number of ways. Housing is one factor that is often used as an indicator of social class. In this case it was uniform for all speakers: at Shinfield the speakers all lived on the Council housing estate, and at the Orts Road playground the speakers all lived in the nearby dilapidated terraced houses. As far as empirical research in Britain is concerned, the criterion most often used to define social class is that of occupation; this has consistently been shown to be related to most other factors associated with social class (see Reid, 1977: 16). At some point during the recording sessions, therefore, speakers were asked about the occupations of their parents. Occasionally this information was elicited from friends rather than from the speakers themselves. The ages of speakers were also ascertained, as was information on their geographical background (since clearly this would affect their use of the local nonstandard variety). The questioning was conducted in an extremely haphazard manner: sometimes the information would be given during a conversation, so that speakers did not need to be asked directly, but sometimes a direct question had to be asked. By the end of nine months the required information had been received for each speaker.

The speakers will be considered as three distinct groups. At the Orts Road playground 10 boys were recorded; these will be considered as a homogeneous group. At the Shinfield playground 3 speakers were boys and 11 were girls. Although they all knew each other (in fact, two were brother and sister), the boys did not normally mix with the girls, and they were never recorded together. These groups, then, will be termed the Shinfield boys group and the Shinfield girls group. The fact that the Shinfield boys group is smaller than the other groups means that at some points in the analysis there is a shortage of contrastive data; this was, however, the natural grouping, and it has the added advantage that the data can be analysed in terms of single-sex groups of speakers. This sex division did not happen by design, but perhaps reflects the tendencies of members of this age group to spend most of their time with friends of the same sex.

2.4.1 Ages of speakers

Age is clearly a significant social factor, since younger children may be less integrated into the peer group culture and may have less systematic patterns of speech; and older children may have begun to acquire adult patterns of style-shifting. Tables 1 and 2 show the ages of the speakers who took part in the recordings. The age range is smaller for female speakers (from 9 to 13, with most girls aged 12, compared with a range of 11 to 17 for male speakers). Some efforts were made to extend the age range for girls by asking younger girls to bring along their older sisters, but this was not a very successful exercise. In any event, the older girls took little part in the activities of the peer group, being more preoccupied with boyfriends and fashion, so their speech would be unlikely to be governed by the norms of the peer group culture.

Although there is a difference in the ages of male and female speakers a statistical analysis of variance showed that this difference is not significant.

Table 1. *Ages of boys*

Name	Age	Name	Age
Orts Road boys		*Shinfield boys*	
Ronny	17	Tommy	15
Ed	16	Pete	14
Rick	16	Dave	13
Smithy	16		
Derek	15		
Alec	15		
Benny	14		
Jeff	13		
Rob	13		
Nobby	11		

Table 2. *Ages of girls*

Name	Age
Sue	13
Valerie	13
Julie	12
Debbie	12
Mandy	12
Tracy	12
Lynne	12
Marlene	11
Ann	10
Christine	10
Sharon	9

2.4.2 Linguistic backgrounds of speakers

Table 3 and Table 4 show the linguistic backgrounds of the speakers. All except two had lived in Reading from the age of two or younger, and most had lived there all their lives. Derek and Rick had moved to Reading from Wales at the age of eight, but since they each had one parent who was from Reading and since there was no discernible Welsh influence on

Table 3. *Linguistic backgrounds of boys*

Name	Years lived in Reading	Place of birth of father	Place of birth of mother
Orts Road boys			
Ronny	17	Reading	Reading
Ed	16	Reading	Reading
Rick	8	Reading	Wales
Smithy	14	Reading	Reading
Derek	7	Reading	Wales
Alec	13	Reading	Reading
Benny	14	Reading	Reading
Jeff	13	Reading	Reading
Rob	13	Germany	Wales
Nobby	11	Reading	Reading
Shinfield boys			
Tommy	15	Reading	Yorkshire
Pete	14	Reading	Reading
Dave	12	Reading	Reading

Table 4. *Linguistic backgrounds of girls*

Name	Years lived in Reading	Place of birth of father	Place of birth of mother
Sue	13	Reading	Yorkshire
Valerie	13	Reading	Reading
Julie	12	?	Reading
Debbie	12	Reading	Reading
Mandy	12	Reading	Reading
Tracy	12	Reading	Reading
Lynne	12	?	Reading
Marlene	11	Reading	Reading
Ann	10	Reading	Reading
Christine	10	Ireland	Reading
Sharon	9	Reading	Reading

their speech (apart from minimal differences in intonation), they were provisionally included in the analysis. In fact, Derek and Rick did not differ significantly from the rest of the group in the frequency with which they used nonstandard linguistic features in their vernacular style. Rob's father was German and his mother Welsh, but this had no discernible effect on Rob's speech. Similarly, although the mother of Tommy and Sue was from Yorkshire (Tommy and Sue were brother and sister), and although Christine's father was from Ireland, this did not appear to affect the speech of these children.

2.4.3 Occupations of parents

The occupations of the children's parents are shown in Tables 5 and 6. The fathers' occupations are all classified under Groups III and IV in the Registrar-General's *Classification of Occupations* (1971). Factors such as having served a full apprenticeship or being self-employed affect classification but could not be taken into account here; even if both these factors were to apply to a given occupation, however, it would not be listed higher than Group III. Perhaps a more relevant consideration is that the fathers' occupations are all manual, which is often taken to be an indication of working-class status.

Where the children's mothers have paid employment their occupations fall into Groups IV and V, except for the occupations of Julie's mother and Marlene's mother, which are classified under Group III.

Table 5. *Occupations of boys' parents*

Name	Occupation of father	Occupation of mother
Orts Road boys		
Ronny	bar staff	bar staff
Ed	motorway construction worker	cleaner
Rick	bricklayer	cleaner
Smithy	car mechanic	cleaner
Derek	distributor	cleaner
Alec	tenant publican	barmaid
Benny	barman	barmaid
Jeff	garage mechanic	telephonist
Rob	welder/sprayer	cleaner
Nobby	slaughterer	barmaid
Shinfield boys		
Tommy	painter/decorator	cleaner
Pete	builder/decorator	cleaner
Dave	car mechanic	canteen assistant

Table 6. *Occupations of girls' parents*

Name	Occupation of father	Occupation of mother
Sue	painter/decorator	cleaner
Valerie	chef	housewife
Julie	(deceased)	typist
Debbie	bus driver	cleaner
Mandy	chef	housewife
Tracy	painter	cleaner
Lynne	? (separated from mother)	canteen assistant
Marlene	lorry driver	cashier
Ann	factory hand	waitress
Christine	factory hand	cleaner
Sharon	glazier	cleaner

Overall, then, the children can be considered as forming a relatively homogeneous social group. Some of their personal characteristics are discussed in Chapter 8.

3 Methods of analysis

The first step in the analysis was to identify the linguistic variables. The number of potential variables is, of course, very large; in this study the field of enquiry will be limited to features that occur in the playground recordings, but that do not occur in standard English. This gives the following list of morphological and syntactic features:

Verb forms
1. Present tense verb forms
2. Past tense verb forms
3. Tense in conditional sentences

Negation
4. *Ain't*
5. Negative concord
6. Nonstandard *never*

Clause syntax
7. Relative pronouns

Nominal constructions
8. Prepositions
9. Demonstrative adjectives
10. Reflexive pronouns
11. Nonstandard *us*
12. Nouns of measurement

Adverbial constructions
13. Comparative adverbs
14. Adverbial forms

Since the playground recordings comprise eighteen hours of spontaneous conversation, it is reasonable to assume that this list includes all the most frequently occurring nonstandard features used by the peer groups. Only morphological and syntactic features are considered in the analysis: this excludes, that is to say, differences of a lexical nature such as the use of *summat* for standard English *something*, or the use of *learn* for standard English *teach*, as in the sentence below:

They don't learn you anything at school (Jeff)

Features that occur only in specific kinds of speech acts are also excluded. This applies in particular to the use of *us* as a first person singular pronoun: *us* occurs with this meaning mainly in requests involving the verb GIVE, or a near equivalent. In the sentence below, for example, Ed was asking for a cigarette for himself and not, as the pronoun might suggest, for himself and some friends:

Lend us a fag, mate (Ed)

It also applies to a few features that are particularly typical of narrative style, such as the use of indefinite *this* to introduce a new topic:

Well, there's this old geezer, right, and he fancies a drink . . . (Rob)

or the use of pronominal apposition:

My brother, he swears like glory, and my mum washed his mouth out with soap and water (Julie)

The morphological and syntactic variables were analysed within the Labovian framework: in other words, each occurrence of the nonstandard form was tabulated for each speaker, together with each occurrence of the corresponding standard English form, and the frequency of occurrence of the nonstandard forms was then expressed as a frequency index, as follows:

$$\text{Frequency index} = \frac{\text{total number of occurrences of nonstandard form}}{\text{total number of occurrences of nonstandard form} + \text{total number of occurrences of standard form}} \times 100$$

A record was kept of the full linguistic context in which each variable form occurred, so that any linguistic constraints on variation could be isolated.

Frequency indices were calculated for individual speakers, and also for each of the three groups of speakers. Group analyses allow a fuller linguistic investigation, since they are based on a larger number of occurrences of variables; for this reason the analysis of linguistic variation in Part II is based entirely on group figures. The indices are calculated as the percentage of the total number of occurrences in the speech of the group as a whole, rather than as the mean of each individual speaker's index, in order to eliminate bias in cases where some speakers use a given feature only rarely (see Trudgill, 1974: 57). Individual analyses, however, can often help to reveal some of the nonlinguistic constraints on variation; much of the sociolinguistic analysis in Part III, therefore, is based either on the speech of individuals or on the speech of small sub-groups within the larger peer group.

Even where analyses are based on group figures, the number of occurrences of a particular variable can sometimes be very low. This is particularly true in the case of the Shinfield boys group, which consists of only three speakers. To some extent, of course, this explains the relative lack of progress that has been made in the study of morphological and syntactic variation: phonological variables are very much easier to analyse, since they occur very frequently even in small stretches of speech. Labov (1972b: 204) suggests that regular patterns of stylistic and social variation emerge even when there are no more than five or ten occurrences of a given variable; this has been taken as a guideline here, and any figures arising from fewer than five occurrences are given in parentheses, to indicate that they may not be typical of group usage. A dash in the Tables indicates that the group of speakers concerned used neither the standard nor the nonstandard form of a given variable, as the variable itself did not occur in the speech of that group during the recordings. Where the number of occurrences of a given feature was low for all groups, statistical tests of significance were performed (if the figures are not statistically significant, this will be indicated in the text).

PART II: LINGUISTIC VARIATION

4 *Verb forms*

4.1 Present tense verb forms

In standard English, present tense verb forms have an -*s* suffix with third person singular subjects only. The suffix has the phonologically conditioned alternants /s, z, ɪz/. In Reading English, as in many other Southwestern varieties, the suffix also occurs with other subjects, as the following examples from the playground recordings illustrate:

> I starts Monday, so shut your face (Rick)
>
> You knows my sister, the one who's small (Rob)
>
> They calls me all the names under the sun, don't they? (Derek)

The nonstandard suffix occurs with most verbs, including the irregular verbs SAY, HAVE and DO. Its occurrence can be attributed to the previous influence of Northern varieties of English: we know that the Northumbrian dialect of Old English, for example, had an -*s* suffix throughout the present tense paradigm, and that this pattern was extended in the Middle English period to Midland areas (Wakelin, 1972: 119–20). We also know that until about 1640 the suffix was used in standard English with singular subjects and occasionally with plural subjects (Strang, 1970: 146), and we can assume that use of the suffix spread to Southwestern varieties of English also. Although the nonstandard forms occur variably, the suffix is categorical with third person singular subjects, as it is in standard English.

Table 7 shows the frequency indices for the nonstandard present tense form (i.e. for suffixed forms with non-third person singular subjects), for each of the three peer groups. The figures are based on 1027 occurrences of regular verbs, plus 66 occurrences of HAVE and 62 of DO. The verbs HAVE and DO are analysed separately, because unlike all other verbs (except BE) they occur with two distinct syntactic functions in sentences: as full verbs, and as auxiliaries. The verb SAY, though irregular, is included in the figures for regular verbs, since like them it occurs only as a full verb.

Table 7 shows clearly that in terms of their overall frequency of occurrence, nonstandard present tense verb forms in Reading English show regular patterns of variation: all three groups of speakers use the nonstandard form most frequently with regular verbs, and least frequently with DO.

Table 7. *Frequency indices for nonstandard -s*

Group	Regular verbs	HAVE	DO
Orts Road boys	50.13	39.29	13.64
Shinfield boys	65.96	(66.67)	25.00
Shinfield girls	52.04	36.00	12.50

4.1.1 Present tense forms of HAVE

HAVE fulfils a number of different syntactic and semantic functions in English. In this analysis we will consider the three most common functions.

In the speech of the peer groups HAVE occurs as a full verb:

> We has a muck around in there (Dave)

> I have a good time with the missis (Ed)

as an auxiliary:

> Well, I have got a boyfriend (Valerie)

> He said, why have you been away? (Sharon)

> They have been down here once (Benny)

and with a following *to-* infinitive, to express obligation:

> You just has to do what these teachers tell you (Mandy)

> Sometimes on Saturdays I has to stop in (Ann)

Table 8 shows the frequency of occurrence of nonstandard forms of HAVE (i.e. of the form *has* with non-third person singular subjects) in these three constructions. (Contracted forms of the auxiliary are included in the analysis.) It can be seen from the Table that the nonstandard form never occurs when HAVE is an auxiliary verb: in other words, auxiliary

Table 8. *Frequency indices for nonstandard* has

Group	Full verb HAVE	HAVE + infinitive	Auxiliary HAVE
Orts Road boys	50.00	71.43	0.00
Shinfield boys	(100.00)	–	0.00
Shinfield girls	51.61	37.93	0.00
All speakers	51.06	39.02	0.00

HAVE has exactly the same forms in Reading English as it has in standard English. The nonstandard forms only occur when HAVE is a full verb, or when it is followed by a *to-* infinitive.

This distribution of the nonstandard forms has clear theoretical implications. For example, it provides empirical evidence concerning the theoretical status of the HAVE plus *to-* infinitive form: this shares the same patterns of variation as the full verb HAVE, and suggests that it should be considered as a full verb, and not as an auxiliary (see Palmer, 1974: 159; Huddleston, 1969: 778). It also provides some empirical evidence for the analysis of auxiliaries as a separate category from full verbs; it has been argued, for example, that the distribution of nonstandard forms in Reading English, and in some other varieties of English, confirms the distinction that can also be made on purely formal grounds between auxiliaries and full verbs (see Palmer, 1979: 7; see also Section 4.1.3).

4.1.2 Linguistic change and HAVE

Relatively little is known about the morphological and syntactic history of regional dialects in Britain. But earlier descriptions of some Southwestern dialects indicate that at one time auxiliary HAVE had a different present tense form from the full verb. Hewett (1892), for example, describes the 'peasant speech' of Devon, and includes HAVE (as *'ave*) in a list of auxiliaries that all have invariant morphological forms in present-day English (including, for example, *will, must, could* and *shall*). Further evidence comes from a nineteenth-century description of the Dorset dialect (Barnes, 1886) which lists *he have* and *he've* as the third person singular forms of the auxiliary paradigm. Another piece of evidence comes from Jane Maxim's tape recordings of older speakers (see Section 1.6): some of these speakers use the form *he have* when HAVE is an auxiliary verb, but they use only *he has* when HAVE is a full verb. Some examples of the auxiliary form are given below:

> I said, but I'll tell you what, I've been allowed to get like this, I said, the doctor have allowed me to get like this (Mrs Ling)

> She said, I never ought to really take Daddy back a present because he haven't written to me, has he? I said, well, he haven't written to you, which I thinks is very mean of him (Mrs Dell)

It is possible, then, that at an earlier stage of the dialect, auxiliary HAVE occurred as *have* with third person singular subjects as well as with other subjects, and that this distinguished it from the full verb HAVE, which would have tended to occur as *has* with all subjects, following the tendency of regular full verbs. We can assume that the distribution of these forms would have gradually changed towards that of the standard English system, where *has* occurs only with third person singular subjects, and where there is no distinction between the auxiliary and the full verb forms. The change appears to have been completed in the auxiliary verb, for, as Table 8 showed, this has the same forms in the speech of the peer groups as it has in standard English, due perhaps to the fact that only one member of the auxiliary paradigm was involved in the change. The full verb, where several members of the paradigm are involved in the change, is still in a state of variation: third person singular forms always occur as *has* (no change has occurred here, of course), but non-third person singular forms occur variably as *has* and *have*. To some extent, then, nonstandard Reading English still makes a morphological distinction between the full verb HAVE and the auxiliary verb HAVE.

4.1.3 Present tense forms of DO

Present tense forms of DO in Reading English are complicated by the fact that there are *three* nonstandard verb forms, which alternate in occurrence with the standard English forms. Firstly, there is a nonstandard suffixed form which occurs with non-third person singular subjects and which is analogous to the nonstandard forms of HAVE and regular verbs:

> Every time we does anything wrong, he sticks you (Tommy)

> That's what I does, anyway, I just ignores them (Sharon)

Secondly, a nonsuffixed form occurs with third person singular subjects:

> But it hurts my dad more than it do her (Mandy)

She cadges, she do (Julie)

Mary, Mary, quite contrary,
How do your garden grow? (Ann)

Finally, the form *dos* (pronounced [duːz]) also occurs, with all subjects, though mostly with third person singular subjects:

All the headmaster dos now is makes you stand in a corner (Nobby)

One bloke stays at home and dos the house-cleaning and all that (Smithy)

Table 9 shows the frequency indices for each of the three nonstandard forms. The analysis is based on the speech of all speakers, in order to provide an adequate number of forms. The distribution of the nonstandard forms in the Table appears erratic: for example, the form *do* occurs

Table 9. *Frequency indices for* does, do *and* dos

Subject	*does*	*do*	*dos*
3rd singular	37.70	52.46	9.84
Non-3rd singular	14.52	83.87	1.61

more often than the other forms, with all subjects, although with third person singular subjects this is a nonstandard form, and with non-third person singular subjects it is the standard form. Some patterns of variation emerge, however, when forms are analysed according to their syntactic function. DO occurs as a full verb:

We does things at school with tape recorders (Mandy)

And all they does is get the shit out (Nobby)

It also occurs as a 'neutral' or 'empty' auxiliary (see Palmer, 1974: 25):

Well, how much do he want for it? (Rick)

Your dad do play cricket, though, don't he? (Benny)

Table 10 shows the frequency indices for each of the three present tense forms, according to their syntactic function.

The distribution of forms now appears more regular. Firstly, we see that the form *dos* occurs only as a full verb (and mostly with third person singular subjects). Secondly, the form *does* occurs more often than the other present tense forms when it is a full verb, with all subjects, even

Table 10. *Frequency indices for* does, do *and* dos *as full verbs and auxiliaries*

Subject	Full verb			Auxiliary		
	does	*do*	*dos*	*does*	*do*	*dos*
3rd singular	50.00	12.50	37.50	33.33	66.67	0.00
Non-3rd singular	56.80	35.70	7.10	2.10	97.90	0.00

though with third person singular subjects this is the standard English form, and with other subjects it is a nonstandard form. And thirdly, the form *do* occurs most frequently when it functions as an auxiliary. Again, the form predominates with all subjects, though it is a nonstandard form when it occurs with third person singular subjects, and a standard form with all other subjects.

It seems, then, that the forms of the verb DO are dependent on different factors in Reading English than in standard English. In standard English the present tense forms of DO depend only on the subject of the verb; in Reading English they also depend on the syntactic function of the verb. Syntactic function, then, is marked in the present tense forms of the verb DO, just as it is in the present tense forms of HAVE.

When auxiliary DO occurs with the negative particle *not,* the use of nonstandard *don't* (i.e. with third person singular subjects) is very high, as Table 11 shows. With non-third person subjects *don't* occurs 100 per cent of the time, as it does in standard English.

Table 11. *Frequency indices for* don't *and* doesn't

Subject	*don't*	*doesn't*
3rd singular	95.20	4.80
Non-3rd singular	100.00	0.00

4.1.4 Linguistic change and DO

As we saw in Section 4.1.2, there is evidence to suggest that at one time auxiliary HAVE and full verb HAVE had different present tense forms.

This may also have been the case for auxiliary and full verb DO. Hewett (1892) includes auxiliary DO (as *dü*) in his list of auxiliary forms in Devon English, and in parts of the West of England there is still a complete distinction between both the present tense forms and the past tense forms of the auxiliary and the full verb (Hughes and Trudgill, 1979). In Reading English the distinction survives intact in the past tense forms (see Section 4.2). However, the distribution of present tense forms suggests that a change is in progress here towards the standard English system. We saw in Table 10, for example, that the form *does* occurs more often than the other forms, with all subjects, when DO is a full verb. This suggests that at one time *does* was the form that was predominantly used throughout the full verb paradigm. The form *do*, however, now occurs 35.7 per cent of the time as a full verb with non-third person singular subjects, presumably because a change towards the standard English paradigm is in progress. *Do* also occurs a small number of times with third person singular subjects, though possibly this is due to hypercorrection. Hypercorrection would also explain the occasional occurrence of non-standard *does* with non-third person singular subjects, when it is an auxiliary.

When DO is an auxiliary, the assumed earlier dialect form, *do,* predominates with all subjects. The fact that this form occurs less often with third person singular subjects than elsewhere indicates, again, that a change is in progress away from the earlier dialect system, where *do* would have been invariant throughout the paradigm, towards the standard English system, where the third person singular form is marked with the *-s* suffix.

The occurrence of the form *dos* would then be seen as a still earlier form of the main verb. In other words, the proposed sequence of present tense forms for the main verb is:

$$dos > does > \begin{cases} does \text{ (3rd singular only)} \\ do \text{ (non-3rd singular)} \end{cases}$$

For the auxiliary verb, the change can be represented as:

$$do > \begin{cases} does \text{ (3rd singular only)} \\ do \text{ (non-3rd singular)} \end{cases}$$

The data from Jane Maxim's recordings of elderly speakers only partially confirm this hypothesis. Table 12 compares the frequency of occurrence of the full verb forms in the speech of the elderly speakers with their

Table 12. *Frequency indices for* does, do *and* dos *as full verbs in the speech of older speakers and younger speakers*

	does		do		dos	
Subject	Older speakers	Younger speakers	Older speakers	Younger speakers	Older speakers	Younger speakers
3rd singular	50.00	50.00	10.00	12.50	40.00	37.50
Non-3rd singular	11.77	56.80	76.46	35.70	11.77	7.10

No. of tokens = 27

frequency in the speech of the peer groups, and Table 13 compares the frequency of occurrence of the auxiliary forms.

Table 12 shows that the older speakers do use the supposedly earlier form *dos* more often than the younger speakers, though the difference is relatively small and the figures are based on a relatively small number of tokens. However, the nonstandard form *does* (i.e. *does* with non-third person singular subjects) is used less often by older speakers than by the younger peer groups; in fact, the older speakers use more standard English full verb forms than the peer groups. Nevertheless, this distribution does not necessarily refute the hypothesis concerning language change. The elderly speakers were recorded in formal interviews, so their speech cannot be directly compared with the informal speech recorded at the adventure playgrounds. We will see in Part III that present tense full verb forms are extremely sensitive indicators of style; they are so sensitive, in fact, that two of the peer group members use no nonstandard forms at all in the school recordings, although they use them quite frequently in the informal playground recordings. We can assume, therefore, that the older speakers might use *does* as a nonstandard full verb form more often in their less formal speech styles; and in fact unsystematic observation of speakers in Reading confirms that *does* is used more often than *do* as a full verb form by adult speakers.

Table 13 shows that older speakers use *do* more often than *does* as an auxiliary form, and that their use of auxiliary *do* is slightly more frequent than that of the peer groups. This, then, appears to confirm the hypothesis that *do* is the older auxiliary form (though again, some caution is needed since the number of tokens is small). The Table also appears to

Table 13. *Frequency indices for* does, do *and* dos *as auxiliaries in the speech of older speakers and younger speakers*

| | *does* | | *do* | | *dos* | |
Subject	Older speakers	Younger speakers	Older speakers	Younger speakers	Older speakers	Younger speakers
3rd singular	28.60	33.33	71.40	66.67	0.00	0.00
Non-3rd singular	0.00	2.10	100.00	97.90	0.00	0.00
No. of tokens = 23						

confirm that *dos* is a full verb and not an auxiliary form, since it is not used as an auxiliary by any speakers.

The empirical evidence for linguistic change is less convincing here, then, than it is for the verb HAVE, but to a large extent this may be due to the fact that the change is as yet incomplete.

4.1.5 Linguistic constraints on regular present tense verb forms

Regular present tense verb forms occur in a number of different linguistic environments. The effect of each of these on the frequency of occurrence of nonstandard present tense forms was analysed in order to identify possible linguistic constraints on variation. Preceding environments were: pronoun, noun, adverb, *who*, *that*, *and*, zero. None of these had a significant effect on the form of the verb. Following environments were: + NP, + NP + relative clause, + prepositional phrase, + complement, zero. A number of characteristics of the verb were also investigated as possible constraints. These were: occurrences in a subordinate clause; time reference (present tense verbs used in order to express the narrative present, repetitive events, durative time and future time); person; and the verb itself (i.e. considered as a lexical item). The effect of the preceding and following phonological segments was also analysed. Two linguistic constraints were isolated; they will each be discussed in turn.

4.1.6 The following complement constraint

The term 'complement' is used here to refer to an embedded sentence that is directly dominated by a present tense verb. The complements used by the peer groups were of the following syntactic types:

1.   V + *-ing*, e.g. I fancies *going over Caversham* (Derek)
2.   infinitive, e.g. I wants *to kill animals* (Nobby)
3.   NP + V, e.g. I just lets *her beat me* (Rick)
4.   *how* + infinitive, e.g. I knows *how to stick in the boot* (Nobby)
5.   *wh-* + S, e.g. Oh, I forget *what the place is called* (Mandy)
6.   *if* + S, e.g. You know *if anything breaks on that pushchair*? (Tommy)
7.   *that* + S, e.g. I believe *that there is, you know, life after death* (Lynne)
8.   + S, e.g. If you're wearing scruffy clothes, they think *you're a bloody hippy* (Debbie)

Complement types 1–4 differ from the other complements in that the subject and tense of the verb in the embedded sentence are not marked in the surface structure of the sentence, and also in that the tense of the embedded verb is co-extensive with the verb in the matrix sentence. In complement types 5–8, the tense of the verb is independent of the matrix verb, and in some cases it may be different from that of the matrix verb, as in the following sentences:

I suppose they went to court (Mandy)

I reckon they should pull our troops out (Derek)

I reckon he always will be the king of rock and roll (Julie)

Table 14 shows the frequency indices for the nonstandard present tense suffixed form when it is followed by each of these two different types of complement. It shows that when a present tense verb is followed by a complement in which the subject and the tense are marked, the nonstandard form rarely or never occurs. Almost all the verbs that precede complements in which tense is marked occur in the nonstandard form in other syntactic environments, which indicates that the form of the complement is the important feature here. Table 15 shows the frequency of occurrence of the nonstandard form when followed by V + *-ing* complements, *to-* infinitive complements and + S complements (the three kinds that occur most frequently in the sample) in the speech of the two larger peer groups. (Figures for the Shinfield boys group were too low to be worth including in the Table.) The frequency of occurrence of the nonstandard form shows a clear relationship with the type of complement

Table 14. *Frequency indices for nonstandard* -s *with following complements*

Group	All verbs	+ complement (tense not marked)	+ complement (tense marked)
Orts Road boys	50.13	47.73	2.63
Shinfield boys	65.96	57.14	0.00
Shinfield girls	52.04	50.00	2.13

that follows: it is highest before a V + *-ing* complement, and lowest before a + S complement.

Table 16 compares the use of nonstandard forms before a following tense marked complement by the peer groups and by the group of elderly speakers. We noted earlier that present tense verb forms are very sensitive to style; this means that we can expect nonstandard forms to be used much less often by the older speakers in interviews than in more informal conversations. Table 16 shows that older speakers in fact use nonstandard verb forms approximately 30 per cent of the time in interviews, so it is not impossible that in informal conversations they would use nonstandard forms more often than the peer groups.

If this were the case, variation in the use of nonstandard verb forms could again be attributed to a linguistic change in progress – a change away from the earlier, uniformly suffixed paradigm towards the standard English system, where only third person singular forms are suffixed. In fact, Table 16 gives an indication of the way in which the change might be proceeding. Younger speakers, as we have seen, rarely use a nonstandard verb form when the verb is the matrix verb of a tense marked complement. Older speakers, however, do use nonstandard verb forms in this

Table 15. *Frequency indices for nonstandard* -s *with following complements*

Group	V + *-ing*	+ infinitive	+ S
Orts Road boys	61.54	33.33	0.00
Shinfield girls	64.71	46.67	2.70

Table 16. *Frequency indices for nonstandard -s in the speech of older speakers and younger speakers*

Group	All verbs	+ complement (tense marked)
Older speakers		
Men	30.61	15.38
Women	31.62	29.17
Younger speakers		
Orts Road boys	50.13	2.63
Shinfield boys	65.96	0.00
Shinfield girls	52.04	2.13

environment, though older men use them less frequently here than elsewhere, as Table 16 shows. This suggests that the change began in a specific linguistic environment, perhaps initially in the speech of men, and that it then saturated that environment relatively quickly – so quickly, in fact, that two generations later speakers only use *nonsuffixed* forms before a tense marked complement.

Table 15 suggests that the change is now spreading to other, related environments – to verbs followed by a *to-* infinitive complement – still, perhaps, led by male speakers, for the Orts Road boys use nonstandard forms less often in this environment than the Shinfield girls.

Clearly, if this is so, it has important implications for theories of diachronic syntax, for it suggests that syntactic changes spread slowly from one environment to another, in much the same way that phonological changes spread gradually across the lexicon. This point will be discussed in more detail in the Conclusion.

4.1.7 The 'vernacular verb' constraint

Some verbs used by the peer groups do not occur in standard English; others are used with a slightly different meaning (often in addition to the standard English one – for example, the verb GO occurs in Reading English with not only its standard English meaning but also the 'vernacular' meaning *say*). A full list of 'vernacular' verbs is given in Table 17. Table 18 shows the frequency of occurrence of nonstandard -*s* with these

Table 17. *'Vernacular' verbs in Reading English*

'Vernacular' verb	Meaning	Example
GO	say	So I goes, oh clear off (Sharon)
CHIN	hit on the chin	We fucking chins them with bottles (Nobby)
BOOT	kick	You boot them, don't you? (Benny)
KILL	beat in a fight	We chins them, we kills them (Rick)
LEG IT	run away	I grabs hold of him and legs it up Blagdon Hill (Tommy)
POKE (nose)	be 'nosey'	Everyone says I pokes my nose, but I don't (Julie)
BUNK	play truant	We bunks it over here a lot (Valerie)
BUS	go by bus	We buses it down the town (Sue)

'vernacular' verbs, compared with the frequency of its occurrence with all regular verbs. It can be seen that the use of a 'vernacular' verb acts as a lexical constraint on the form of the verb, strongly favouring the nonstandard form.

Lexical constraints such as this, of course, are of a different nature from the syntactic constraint described in the previous section. The effect of a syntactic constraint would not be expected to vary with speech style, since the use of an auxiliary rather than a main verb, for example, or the use of a following finite complement is independent of style. The effect of a lexical constraint, however, would tend to vary with style, for the choice of a particular lexical item, such as a 'vernacular' verb, is closely linked to the extralinguistic situation. The predominance of nonstandard -*s* with 'vernacular' verbs suggests that the use of nonstandard features may have a cumulative effect: if a nonstandard lexical item is a feature that can occur in a nonstandard morphological form, then the probability that it will occur in the nonstandard form is very high.

Table 18. *Frequency indices for nonstandard -s with 'vernacular' verbs*

Group	All verbs	'Vernacular' verbs
Orts Road boys	50.13	94.29
Shinfield boys	65.96	90.00
Shinfield girls	52.04	95.56

4.2 Past tense verb forms

4.2.1 Past tense forms of BE

In standard English, past tense forms of BE differ from all other past tense verb forms by having more than one morphological form: *was* is used with first and third person singular subjects, and *were* is used elsewhere. Many other varieties of English have a more regular past tense system: in Bradford, for example, the form *were* occurs, with all persons (Hughes and Trudgill, 1979: 60). In Reading English the form *was* is used not only with first and third person singular subjects, as it is in standard English, but also with other subjects, as in the examples below:

> Wasn't we more greasers than we was skinheads? (Pete)

> You was with me, wasn't you? (Ann)

> The coppers let him go to the van to see if they was the bastards (Nobby)

Past tense forms of BE occur 712 times in the recordings.

Table 19 shows the frequency of occurrence of nonstandard *was*. Although the nonstandard form occurs less often in the girls' speech than in the boys', there is a clear overall tendency for speakers to use a single past tense form, *was*, throughout the paradigm.

Table 19. *Frequency index for nonstandard* was

Group	Frequency index
Orts Road boys	89.58
Shinfield boys	86.11
Shinfield girls	73.58
All speakers	83.19

A nonstandard form, *were*, occurs also, with first and third person singular subjects:

> Hardest kid in the school there, weren't I? (Alec)

> 'Cos I were going to smash him up, and he had to get Rick (Derek)

The use of *were* is infrequent, however, as Table 20 shows.

Table 20. *Frequency index for*
nonstandard were

Group	Frequency index
Orts Road boys	7.79
Shinfield boys	0.00
Shinfield girls	2.64
All speakers	3.97

The occurrence of the negative particle *not* or *n't* has an interesting effect on the nonstandard forms. Table 21 shows that *were* occurs more often when the negative particle is present than when it is not (except in the Shinfield boys' speech, where data are limited, and therefore unreliable). This is so with all subjects, though with first and third person singular subjects *weren't* is a nonstandard form, and elsewhere it is the standard form.

No other constraints affect the past tense forms of BE: the distinction between the auxiliary verb and the full verb, for example, which was marked in forms of HAVE and DO, does not seem to be relevant here. Again, though, the forms of the verb in Reading English and in standard English differ in their choice of marking. In standard English the subject of the verb is marked, in that *was* occurs with first and third person singular subjects, and *were* with other subjects. In Reading English it is negation that is marked, though marking is variable: when the verb is negated, there is an increased use of *weren't*, with all subjects, and when the verb is not negated, the form *was* tends to occur with all subjects. Older speakers did not use past tense forms of BE often enough for a

Table 21. *Frequency indices for* were

Group	1st and 3rd singular subjects Nonstandard *were*	Nonstandard *weren't*	1st, 2nd, 3rd plural subjects Standard *were*	Standard *weren't*
Orts Road boys	0.75	52.38	9.89	20.00
Shinfield boys	0.00	0.00	8.82	(0.00)
Shinfield girls	0.92	36.36	25.00	60.00
All speakers	0.73	36.59	16.29	41.18

comparative analysis to be made, and there seems to be no evidence available concerning earlier dialect forms (the *Survey of English Dialects,* as we saw earlier, does not, unfortunately, provide comparable data). No conclusions regarding linguistic change can be drawn, therefore, although it seems probable that the use of *were* with a negative particle is a relic of an earlier dialect form.

4.2.2 Other past tense forms

It will be useful to review briefly the past tense forms that occur in standard English before considering the forms that are used by the peer groups.

In standard English the past tense is formed in one of two ways. The suffix *-ed* (realised phonologically as /d/, /t/ or /ɪd/) may be added to the verb stem, as with *jump–jumped*; *laugh–laughed*; *hunt–hunted*. (Some verbs have differing realisations, such as *learnt–learned*; *dreamt–dreamed*.) Alternatively, a vowel change may take place within the verb stem, as with *come–came*; *light–lit*. In contemporary English most verbs now form their past tense by means of the *-ed* suffix, and verbs that form their past tense in this way usually have this same form as the past participle, as below:

Stem	Past tense form	Past participle form
jump	I jumped	I have jumped
dance	I danced	I have danced
laugh	I laughed	I have laughed

Some verbs that form their past tense by means of a vowel change also have identical past tense and past participle forms:

Stem	Past tense form	Past participle form
sit	I sat	I have sat
say	I said	I have said
light	I lit	I have lit

Others have different past tense and past participle forms. Some past participle forms are identical to the verb stem:

Stem	Past tense form	Past participle form
run	I ran	I have run
come	I came	I have come

Other past participle forms have the suffix *-en* added to the verb stem:

Stem	Past tense form	Past participle form
see	I saw	I have seen
give	I gave	I have given
drive	I drove	I have driven

or to the past tense form:

Stem	Past tense form	Past participle form
forget	I forgot	I have forgotten
break	I broke	I have broken
steal	I stole	I have stolen

In Reading English the past tenses and past participles are also formed by these methods, but sometimes the method used for a given verb differs from the method used in standard English.

For example, eight verbs which in standard English form the past tense by means of a vowel change occur in the peer group data with an *-ed* past tense suffix. These verbs are GIVE, HOLD, DRAW, SWING, RUN, BLOW, FIGHT and WAKE. Some examples follow:

> It was just the floor what blowed up (Sharon)

> The baby was teething and I couldn't get no sleep, it woked everyone up (Mandy)

> How much money have you hold, held, holded in your hand? (Rob)

The form *woked,* in Mandy's sentence, has the *-ed* suffix added to the standard English past tense form; the other seven forms all have the *-ed* suffix added to the verb stem. The verbs FIGHT and DRAW also occur with past participles formed by the addition of the *-ed* suffix:

> I've never fighted with her (Sharon)

> I wants to see how you've drawed the wings (Ann)

Some verbs that form their past tense by means of a vowel change have different past tense and past participle forms in standard English; in Reading English these verbs sometimes have identical past tense and past participle forms. The verbs GO, TAKE, FORGET, RUN, BREAK, THROW, BEAT and SEE, for example, have the standard English past tense form as both past tense and past participle forms in the recordings:

> And if we'd went to court I'd probably have got done, done more than what he got done (Dave)

No I ain't, I've been and forgot it again (Ronny)

I'd have ran out there and spat in her face (Julie)

The verbs COME, BECOME, RUN (again) and full verb DO have the standard English past participle form for both the past tense and past participle forms:

I done the most to him, mate, I half killed him (Dave)

You run away though, didn't you? (Tommy)

The nonstandard past tense form *done* deserves special comment, for the traditional distinction between auxiliary DO and full verb DO is preserved in the past tense forms, with *done* occurring categorically as the past tense full verb form, and *did* occurring categorically as the past tense auxiliary form, as in the sentence below:

She done it, didn't she, Tracy? (Mandy)

This distinction does not, of course, exist in standard English, where the form *did* is used for both the full verb and the auxiliary (see Hughes and Trudgill, 1979: 16).

The past tense system in Reading English is complicated by the fact that the same verb sometimes occurs in more than one past tense form. For example, there are two separate past tense forms for the verb RUN, as we have seen. GIVE and SEE occur in past tense forms that are identical to the verb stem, as well as in the forms noted earlier:

Yeah, we peeped in the tent and we see him fingering her (Jeff)

My mum give him a towel (Nobby)

The verbs STRING UP and SHIT also occur in past tense forms that are identical to the verb stem.

Finally, the verb DRIVE occasionally occurs with the past participle form *driv*, as in the sentence below:

I've driv that from there over here (Tommy)

This appears to be formed by the same kind of vowel change that produces the past tense form *lit* for the verb LIGHT, and the nonstandard past tense form *writ* (overheard in the town) for the verb WRITE.

The verbs SEE, COME and DO (full verb) are the only verbs that occur frequently enough in the data for their frequency indices to be calculated. Frequency indices for the nonstandard past tense forms *see* and *come* are shown in Table 22. The nonstandard past tense form *seen*,

Table 22. *Frequency indices for non-standard past tense forms* see *and* come

Group	*see*	*come*
Orts Road boys	81.82	100.00
Shinfield boys	100.00	100.00
Shinfield girls	44.44	73.33

which is very common in areas farther west than Reading, as well as in London, was also used by the peer groups, as was the standard English form *saw*; *see*, however, was by far the most frequently used form. The nonstandard past tense form *done*, as already noted, was used 100 per cent of the time by all speakers. The figures in the Table exclude cases where a non-third person singular form occurs in a narrative, in order to avoid the possibility of counting narrative present forms such as *I see, they come* as past tense forms. It can be seen that nonstandard forms occur very frequently in the boys' speech, but less frequently in the girls' speech.

With the exception of *done*, nonstandard past tense forms occur variably with their standard English equivalent forms. This variation did not, however, appear to be governed by any linguistic constraints. The main point of interest in the Reading English past tense system, then, lies in the greater regularity of the past tense verb forms, compared to the standard English forms. Most English verbs now form their past tense forms by means of the -*ed* suffix, as we have seen, and Reading English extends this historical process to verbs that are irregular in standard English. Similarly, most English verbs have the same form for the past tense and the past participle; in Reading English this more common pattern applies to verbs that in standard English have different forms.

4.3 Tense in conditional sentences

The tense of the verb in conditional sentences referring to past time is not the same in Reading English as it is in standard English. In standard English the verb in the subordinate clause is usually in the past perfect tense and the verb in the main clause in the 'conditional' tense (i.e. with *would*), as in the sentence:

> If he'd wanted to win, he would have tried harder

Twelve past tense conditional sentences occur in the peer group recordings. This is too small a number to allow a full analysis, but it is worth noting that none of these sentences has the same form as the standard English conditional sentence. One has no 'conditional' verb in either clause:

> But if we was come in any later than half past ten, we will get into trouble (Valerie)

Four sentences have a preterite verb in the subordinate clause:

> He looked up, that's it, and if he didn't look up, it'd have caught him in the eye (Tommy)

One sentence has the form *had have* in the subordinate clause:

> I cut the tendon in my big toe, and if I hadn't have gone to the hospital when I did, I wouldn't have got there at all (Derek)

Six sentences have conditional verbs in both clauses, as in the sentences below:

> If she would have drowned, she wouldn't have been a witch (Rick)

> If they wouldn't have waited, she would have had a go at them (Nobby)

In one of these sentences the verb in the subordinate clause is contracted and may, therefore, be derived either from *had have* (as in Derek's sentence, above) or from *would have*:

> If I'd have known he'd have run, I would have run (Dave)

In five sentences, however, the full form *would have* is used. Petyt (1977: 313–14) notes that the contracted form [dəv] occurs in conditional clauses in the industrial West Riding, and suggests that at one time the full form may have been *would have* (as it is in conditional sentences in American English), rather than standard English *had have*. Our data suggest that this may be true for Reading English also.

When conditional sentences refer to present time, however, the verbs have the same tense as in standard English:

> Well, if we had a better Reading team, we'd more than likely go and see her (Nobby)

5 Negation

5.1 *Ain't*

Ain't is an extremely widespread feature of English, probably occurring in all nonstandard American English varieties (Wolfram and Fasold, 1974: 162) and in most British English varieties. It functions in three distinct ways: as the present tense negative form of auxiliary BE, the present tense negative form of the BE copula, and the present tense negative form of auxiliary HAVE (but not of full verb HAVE); in each case, it occurs with all persons of the verb. In the Black English Vernacular it also occurs as a variant of *didn't* (see, for example, Wolfram, 1973: 154).

The sentences below provide examples of the occurrence of *ain't* in the peer group recordings:

> *Ain't* = aux. BE + *not*
>
> How come that ain't working? (Benny)
>
> Course I ain't going to the Avenue (Mandy)
>
> *Ain't* = copula BE + *not*
>
> You ain't no boss (Rob)
>
> We've got a park near us, but there ain't nothing over there (Julie)
>
> *Ain't* = aux. HAVE + *not*
>
> I ain't got one single flea in my hair, they're all married (Rob)
>
> What do you expect, you ain't been round there, have you? (Ronny)

Negative present tense forms of HAVE + *not* and BE + *not* occurred 439 times in the recordings. Table 23 shows the frequency indices for *ain't*. Its occurrence follows a regular pattern, with *ain't* occurring most often as auxiliary HAVE, in the speech of all groups, and least often as auxiliary BE. In each case the girls use *ain't* less often than the boys.

Table 23. *Frequency indices for* ain't

Group	*ain't =* aux. HAVE + *not*	*ain't =* copula BE + *not*	*ain't =* aux. BE + *not*
Orts Road boys	91.18	84.16	79.07
Shinfield boys	100.00	94.74	63.16
Shinfield girls	65.58	61.18	42.11

5.1.1 Standard English forms

The standard English forms that correspond to *ain't* are the present tense forms of BE or HAVE, with the particle *not*: i.e. *am not, are not, is not, have not* and *has not*. In colloquial standard English these forms are normally abbreviated, either by assimilation of the verb to a preceding subject (termed the 'uncontracted negative' in Quirk et al., 1972):

> You're not going anywhere (Sharon)

or by reduction and assimilation of the particle to the preceding verb:

> You aren't a virgin (Tommy)

The uncontracted forms are preferred by the peer groups for forms of BE: in the recordings they occur 100 per cent of the time for auxiliary BE + *not*, and 74 per cent of the time for the copula BE + *not*. This preference is surprising, for the uncontracted forms are usually considered more typical of Northern and Scottish varieties of English (see, for example, Hughes and Trudgill, 1979). Auxiliary HAVE, however, always occurs in the contracted negative form, so in this case Reading English follows the general tendency of Southern English varieties to prefer the contracted form.

5.1.2 Linguistic constraints on *ain't*

In the recordings made at the playgrounds *ain't* occurs in declarative sentences, in interrogative sentences and in tag questions:

> I ain't seen my nan for nearly seven years (Tracy)
>
> Oh, ain't you clever? (Pete)
>
> Lustful Vicar, we've had that one, ain't we? (Rick)

Table 24 shows the frequency indices for *ain't* in declarative sentences and in tag questions. Negative present tense contracted forms of HAVE and BE occur only rarely in interrogative sentences, and these are not, therefore, included in the analysis. It can be seen from the Table that the frequency of occurrence of *ain't* in tag questions is consistently higher than its frequency of occurrence in declarative sentences: in some cases it occurs 100 per cent of the time.

Table 24. *Frequency indices for* ain't *in declarative sentences and tag questions*

Verb form	Group	Declarative sentences	Tag questions
Auxiliary HAVE	Orts Road boys	88.68	100.00
	Shinfield boys	100.00	(100.00)
	Shinfield girls	62.50	80.00
	All speakers	78.57	95.00
Copula BE	Orts Road boys	68.00	100.00
	Shinfield boys	92.31	100.00
	Shinfield girls	44.44	89.66
	All speakers	59.83	96.30
Auxiliary BE	Orts Road boys	76.67	100.00
	Shinfield boys	60.00	(75.00)
	Shinfield girls	31.25	(66.67)
	All speakers	60.66	88.89

5.1.3 Derivation of *ain't*

As we have seen, the single form *ain't* corresponds to a number of standard English forms: *(a)m not, aren't, isn't, hasn't* and *haven't*. The tendency to use one form throughout a verbal paradigm is typical of nonstandard dialects, and this has been illustrated by many of the features considered so far. It is unusual, however, for a single form to be used for two verbs that have distinct syntactic functions, and it is worth looking at the derivation of *ain't*, therefore, in search of an explanation.

A full discussion of the derivation of *ain't* is given in Cheshire (1981a); this concludes that the use of the one form *ain't* for the negative present tense contracted forms of both HAVE and BE is simply the result of a diachronic coincidence. Jespersen (1940: 430–1) and Stevens (1954: 200), for example, show how *ain't* could have been derived by regular sound change from both *haven't* and *hasn't*, through loss of the initial aspirate and the fricative, and diphthongisation of the long vowel used in these negative forms (which at one time may have distinguished them from the non-negative forms). These writers also show how *am not* could have yielded the Early Modern English form [ænt], by assimilation of the first nasal to the second and lengthening of the vowel, followed by diphthongisation to produce [eɪnt]. *Ain't* could also have been derived independently from standard English *aren't* and *isn't* (see Jespersen, 1940: 431–3), but there is little evidence to substantiate this, and the more likely explanation is that the form [eɪnt] was extended from use with first person singular subjects to use with other subjects, by analogy with the other negative present tense contracted forms which have a single form throughout the paradigm (such as, for example, *can't* and *won't*).

5.1.4 Phonetic realisations of *ain't*

The discussion so far has used the general term *ain't* to refer to all nonstandard realisations of the negative present tense contracted forms of the copula BE and of the auxiliaries BE and HAVE. In reality, however, the nonstandard variant has a range of phonetic realisations. *The Linguistic Atlas of England* (Orton, Sanderson and Widdowson, 1978) gives *ain't*, *en't* and *ben't* as nonstandard forms found in rural Berkshire; in the peer group recordings, however, the nonstandard forms that are used fall into two main groups: those that approximate to *ain't* (including [eɪnt], [eɪn], [eɪʔ], [eɪ̄], [eɪ̄ʔ], [ɛnt] and [æn]) and those that have a higher vowel and approximate more closely to *in't* (including [ɪn], [ī] and [ɪnt]).

Since *ain't* is assumed to be derived from the standard English verb forms, it is reasonable to expect that a realisation as *in't* would occur only only with third person singular subjects of the copula or of auxiliary BE – to expect, in other words, that nonstandard *in't* would correspond to standard English *isn't,* and nonstandard *ain't* to the other standard English forms (*(a)m not, aren't, hasn't* and *haven't*). In fact, however, the distribution is more complex than this, as Table 25 shows. The indices for the Shinfield boys group show the distribution that would be expected if nonstandard *in't* corresponded to standard *isn't: in't* does not occur as the negative auxiliary HAVE, nor does it occur with non-third person singu-

Table 25. *Frequency indices for* in't

$$\left(\frac{\text{no. of } in't \text{ forms}}{\text{no. of } in't + \text{no. of } ain't \text{ forms}} \times 100\right)$$

Group	Auxiliary HAVE 3rd Singular subjects	Other subjects	Copula BE 3rd Singular subjects	Other subjects	Auxiliary BE 3rd Singular subjects	Other subjects
Orts Road boys	24.00	8.33	63.24	41.67	50.00	15.38
Shinfield boys	(0.00)	(0.00)	33.33	0.00	(66.67)	0.00
Shinfield girls	0.00	0.00	61.54	10.00	(50.00)	(25.00)
All speakers	16.22	5.17	60.34	19.35	53.85	12.82

lar subjects of the negative copula and auxiliary BE. The Shinfield group consists of only three speakers, however, which means that the analysis is based on a small number of tokens. The figures for the other groups of speakers are based on a more substantial number of forms, and here the use of *in't* is more widespread: both groups use *in't* for BE with subjects that are *not* third person singular, and the Orts Road boys use *in't* with auxiliary HAVE also.

It is relevant at this point to consider the effect of tag questions on negative present tense forms. Tag questions, as we saw earlier (Section 5.1.2), strongly favour the use of a nonstandard form; but we have not yet established whether the nonstandard form is *in't* or *ain't* (or, indeed, both). Table 26, then, gives the frequency indices for *ain't, in't* and the corresponding standard English forms, with third person singular subjects, both in declarative sentences and in tag questions. Table 27 gives the indices for these same forms, with subjects that are not third person singular. In both Tables the figures represent the total use of each form by all speakers. (A full version of the Tables, giving the breakdown for each of the three peer groups, can be found in the Appendix. Group figures show the same distribution of forms, except that with third person singular subjects the girls use the standard English contracted forms more often than either *ain't* or *in't*.)

Table 26 shows that although *in't* forms occur more often with the verb BE and a third person singular subject, as would be expected if *in't* corresponded to standard English *isn't*, these occurrences are almost

Table 26. *Frequency indices for* ain't, in't *and standard English forms with third person singular subjects*

Verb form	Declarative sentences			Tag questions		
	ain't	*in't*	*hasn't*	*ain't*	*in't*	*hasn't*
Auxiliary HAVE	82.35	0.00	17.65	33.33	66.67	0.00
	ain't	*in't*	*isn't*	*ain't*	*in't*	*isn't*
Copula BE	54.32	6.17	39.51	2.86	92.86	4.28
Auxiliary BE	50.00	8.33	41.67	0.00	85.71	14.29

entirely in tag questions. In declarative sentences the form *ain't* predominates, for all verbs, and *in't* occurs only rarely (as the copula and auxiliary BE, and not as auxiliary HAVE). In tag questions this distribution is reversed, with *in't* now predominating, for all verbs, and *ain't* now occurring less often as auxiliary HAVE, and rarely or never as the copula or auxiliary BE.

Table 27 shows that these tendencies persist when the subject is non-third person singular. If the nonstandard forms corresponded to the standard English forms, *in't* would not occur in this Table. In fact, however, *in't* is again the predominant form in tag questions when the verb is the copula or auxiliary BE, and it also occurs, though to a more limited extent, when the verb in the tag question is auxiliary HAVE. In declarative sentences, *ain't* is the only nonstandard form that is used, for all verbs.

Clearly, then, the nonstandard forms *ain't* and *in't* do not stand in a simple relationship to the standard English negative present tense contracted forms. They do bear *some* relationship to the standard English forms, for *in't* forms occur less often with the verb HAVE than with the verb BE; and in the environment that can be considered the furthest removed from *in't* (the verb HAVE with a non-third person singular subject), *ain't,* rather than *in't,* is the preferred form in tag questions (though even here *in't* occurs 27.27 per cent of the time). There is an overall tendency in Reading English, however, for nonstandard *ain't* to be used in declarative sentences, and for nonstandard *in't* to be used in tag questions.

It is worth noting that the tendency to use *in't* as an invariant form in tag

Table 27. *Frequency indices for* ain't, in't *and standard English forms with non-third person singular subjects*

Verb form	Declarative sentences			Tag questions		
	ain't	*in't*	*haven't*	*ain't*	*in't*	*haven't*
Auxiliary HAVE	76.56	0.00	23.44	72.73	27.27	0.00
	ain't	*in't*	*aren't*	*ain't*	*in't*	*aren't*
Copula BE	58.33	0.00	41.67	40.00	60.00	0.00
Auxiliary BE	61.22	0.00	38.78	44.44	55.56	0.00

questions is not confined to Reading English. In the variety of English spoken in Edinburgh, for example, *in't* also occurs with all subjects of the verb BE (see Brown and Millar, 1978: 172).

5.1.5 Semantic functions of tag questions

Tag questions occur frequently in the peer group recordings, particularly in the boys' speech. Most of them are used to seek confirmation of an offered fact:

He lives here, doesn't he? (Ed)

to seek corroboration:

My brother carried him all the way down the hospital, didn't he? (Nobby)

or to seek support for an opinion:

Well, it is rude, isn't it? (Pete)

The characteristic intonation of the tag question is either a fall-rise (as in Ed's tag) or a fall (as in Nobby's and Pete's tags). Speakers usually have a particular answer in mind, and they expect an answer to be given. This accords with what is usually considered to be the function of tag questions in standard English: to seek confirmation or corroboration for the hopes or suppositions expressed in the sentence to which they are attached. The tag questions conform to a proposed deep structure semantic condition (or 'sincerity condition') to which all questions, including tagged declaratives, are subject: the speaker believes that the hearer knows at least as well as he does whether the proposition he is expressing is true (see Hudson, 1975: 11).

There are a number of tag questions in the recordings, however, that do not expect the hearer to confirm the proposition of the main sentence and that, furthermore, do not conform to the sincerity condition for interrogative sentences. The exchange below provides an example:

Julie:	We're going to Southsea on the 17th of next month. And on Sunday they –
Debbie:	Yeah, and I can't bloody go.
Jenny:	Why not?
Debbie:	'Cos I'm going on fucking holiday, in I?

No answer was expected to this tag question, and it would in any case have been impossible to provide one, since I had no way of knowing when Debbie was going on holiday. Furthermore, she knew that I did not know, so the sincerity condition for interrogative sentences does not apply here: the speaker believes that the proposition in the main sentence is true, but she does not believe that the hearer knows whether it is true or false. This may account for the assertive and aggressive overtones that this type of tag conveys; in any case, the function of the tag question here is not to seek confirmation, but to express aggression.

Tag questions of this type seem mostly to occur in working-class speech. A further type of tag question, however, whose occurrence is perhaps more widespread, is used by the peer groups as a way of provoking a fight or an argument. A falling intonation is normally used. An example is:

You're a fucking hard nut, in't you? (Ed)

No verbal answer was expected here, but a physical one may well have been, for in response to Ed's question the hearer jumped on him and threw him to the ground. It is difficult to establish whether the sincerity condition for interrogative sentences is fulfilled here or not: Ed may not really believe that his friend is a 'hard nut', but may believe it only temporarily, or may be pretending to believe it in order to start a fight; and his assumptions about the hearer's beliefs are equally unclear. Again, though, the function of the tag question is clearly not to seek confirmation, but to convey aggression.

Broadly speaking, then, the tag questions used by the peer groups fall into two groups: a larger group, where tags have the more usual function of requiring confirmation or corroboration, and where Hudson's sincerity condition is fulfilled; and a smaller group, consisting of tags that do not require an answer, that do not seem to fulfil the sincerity condition for questions and that express assertion and aggression.

Table 28 shows the number of times that *in't*, *ain't* and the standard English forms are used by the peer groups in each of these two types of tag. Tag type 1 consists of 'conventional' tags (i.e. tags seeking confirmation), and Tag type 2 consists of 'unconventional' tags. The Table reveals that there is a different distribution of verb forms in these two types of tag, for *in't* occurs in both types, whereas *ain't* and the standard English forms occur only in 'conventional' tags. In other words, the use of *in't* is categorical in 'unconventional' tags, but variable in 'conventional' tags.

Why should the nonstandard forms be semantically marked in this way? One explanation may lie in the fact that there is a common feature in the semantic function of 'unconventional' tags and in the vernacular culture to which the peer groups belong. 'Unconventional' tags, as we

Table 28. *Number of occurrences of* ain't, in't *and standard English forms in different types of tag questions*

| | 3rd singular subjects | | | | | |
Verb form	Tag type 1			Tag type 2		
	ain't	*in't*	*hasn't*	*ain't*	*in't*	*hasn't*
Auxiliary HAVE	3	6	0	0	0	0
	ain't	*in't*	*isn't*	*ain't*	*in't*	*isn't*
Copula BE	2	59	3	0	5	0
Auxiliary BE	0	3	1	0	3	0
Total	5	68	4	0	8	0

| | Non-3rd singular subjects | | | | | |
Verb form	Tag type 1			Tag type 2		
	ain't	*in't*	*haven't*	*ain't*	*in't*	*haven't*
Auxiliary HAVE	7	1	1	0	2	0
	ain't	*in't*	*aren't*	*ain't*	*in't*	*aren't*
Copula BE	1	5	0	0	1	0
Auxiliary BE	4	1	0	0	4	0
Total	12	7	1	0	7	0
COMBINED TOTAL (all subjects)	17	75	5	0	15	0

have seen, express hostility, assertion or aggression. These are recurrent themes within the peer group culture: for example, prestige within the group is achieved through success in fighting, shoplifting, arson and vandalism, all of which are aggressive, assertive acts. The extent to which speakers participate in the vernacular culture is directly linked to the frequency with which they use many of the nonstandard features of Reading English, as we will see later; interestingly, however, *ain't* is one of the few features that are not correlated in this way with vernacular culture. It seems, instead, that there may be a more indirect link between *ain't* and the vernacular culture: when the feature occurs in an 'unconventional' tag, which carries overtones of aggression and hostility, the form *in't* is categorical. In other words, when tag questions directly express a dominant theme of the vernacular culture, *in't* is used as an invariant verb form; in all other environments *in't* is variable, alternating in occurrence with *ain't* and the standard English forms.

This phenomenon is not unknown in language. In his discussion of negative concord in the Black English Vernacular, Labov (1972d: 804) gives an example of a cultural feature (lack of 'booklearning') which coincides with the use of nonstandard grammar. And Hudson (1975: 14–15) argues that the *n't* that occurs in exclamations of the kind:

> Hasn't he done well!

is not a reflex of the deep structure formative NEG, as it is in questions such as:

> Hasn't he done it yet?

(though presumably it was at some earlier stage), but is instead a marker of 'exclamation' related to the negative form *n't* only in morphological form. Hudson points to other syntactic splits of this kind in English, such as that between the full verb OWE and the modal OUGHT, where *ought* was at one time the past tense form of OWE. The *in't* that occurs as an invariant form in 'unconventional' tag questions may, similarly, be related only historically to the third person singular form *isn't,* and instead may now be a marker of the vernacular themes of aggression and hostility – a 'force marker' (see Hudson, 1975: 10).

In fact, it seems that it is not just the form *in't,* but the 'unconventional' tag question as a whole, that functions as the force marker. 'Unconventional' tags do not function in the same way as 'conventional' tags. They do not, for example, have the same semantic or pragmatic properties:

they do not conform to Hudson's sincerity condition, nor do they require the hearer to confirm the proposition of the main clause. They do not have the same syntactic properties as 'conventional' tag questions, either: 'conventional' tags repeat the subject and verb of the main clause, but in 'unconventional' tags the form *in't* may correspond to non-third person singular forms of BE, or even to forms of HAVE. There are a few sentences in the recordings where the subject and verb in the 'unconventional' tag are still further removed from those of the main sentence:

She's too good for you, in it? (Smithy)

She makes her laugh, in it? (Julie)

In Smithy's sentence the verb in the main sentence is repeated in the tag, but the subject is not; in Julie's sentence, the subject is not repeated in the tag, and the form *in* is used in place of 'empty' DO.

5.1.6 Continuing linguistic change in the form of *ain't*

We saw earlier (Section 5.1.3) that the phonetic variants of the nonstandard form have been explained traditionally as the result of the processes of phonetic change and morphological analogy. The form *in't* is assumed to be derived by phonetic change from standard English *isn't,* and the form *ain't* from *hasn't* and *haven't,* as well as from one (or more) of the negative present tense forms of BE, spreading throughout the paradigm by morphological analogy.

The older speakers in Maxim's sample did not use a large number of negative present tense forms of HAVE and BE, as Table 29 shows. (The figures in the Table are based on only 41 occurrences of the variable.) The Table does suggest, however, that older speakers use *in't* only as a third person singular form of the verb BE: in other words, only as an equivalent to the standard form *isn't.* Elsewhere it seems that either *ain't* or the standard forms are preferred. The fact that adolescent speakers use *in't* in other environments, then, suggests that a change in the use of *in't* has occurred over two generations of speakers. If we analyse the speech of the peer groups in more detail, it is possible to obtain some understanding of the mechanism of the change. In the peer group recordings, third person singular forms of BE account for 78 per cent of the verb forms in 'conventional' tag questions. This means that in tag questions the form *in't* occurs more often than any other verb form, since this is the preferred form in tags for third person singular forms of BE (see Table 26). It is

Table 29. *Frequency indices for* ain't, in't *and standard English forms in the speech of older speakers*

Verb	Declarative sentences			Tag questions		
		3rd singular subjects				
HAVE	*ain't* (66.67)	*in't* –	*hasn't* (33.33)	*ain't* –	*in't* –	*hasn't* –
BE	*ain't* (100.00)	*in't* –	*isn't* –	*ain't* –	*in't* 33.33	*isn't* 66.67
		Non-3rd singular subjects				
HAVE	*ain't* 41.67	*in't* –	*haven't* 58.33	*ain't* 33.33	*in't* –	*haven't* 66.67
BE	*ain't* (50.00)	*in't* –	*aren't* (50.00)	*ain't* –	*in't* –	*aren't* (100.00)

highly probable, therefore, that as a result of its frequent occurrence in tag questions, *in't* would begin to occur in this environment with subjects other than third person singular subjects, and with auxiliary HAVE as well as with BE. In other words, what may be happening here is precisely what is presumed to have happened at an earlier stage of English to the form *ain't* – a form that occurs very frequently in colloquial speech as one member of a morphological paradigm spreads throughout the rest of the paradigm. We can predict that *in't* will gradually replace *ain't* as the nonstandard form.

If this hypothesis is correct, the data provide further evidence that morphological change begins in one syntactic environment before spreading to other areas of the language. In this case it is possible to guess at the state of progress of the change by noting the different frequencies with which *in't* occurs in the peer group recordings. Table 26 suggests that the change is further advanced with third person singular forms of HAVE, for *in't* occurs 66.67 per cent of the time here. This may well be due to the fact that third person singular subjects occur more often than other subjects. Table 27 indicates that the change is also spreading to non-third person singular forms of BE, and that it is beginning to affect non-third person singular forms of HAVE.

The fact that *in't* appears to have become an overt marker of a vernacular norm would seem to be unconnected with the change; *in't* functions in this way only in 'unconventional' tags, which, as we have seen, cannot be considered as true tag questions, since they have neither the semantic nor the syntactic properties of tags.

5.2 Negative concord

Negative concord occurs when a negative element is realised at two or more places in a sentence, as in the following examples:

> That's where we go clubbing when there ain't nothing to do (Jeff)

> It ain't got no pedigree or nothing (Nobby)

> I wouldn't let him touch me nowhere (Brenda)

The majority of languages, including most of the nonstandard varieties of American English and British English, use this method of negation. The standard English method of negation was imposed on the language by grammarians in the eighteenth century, with the result that today standard English clauses contain only one negative element, which occurs either with the verb:

> There isn't any hope

or, less frequently and somewhat more emphatically, with the indeterminate immediately following the verb:

> There is no hope

Where two negatives occur in a standard English clause the meaning is no longer negative, as the following hypothetical example illustrates:

> I don't want anything [i.e. I want nothing]

> I don't want nothing [i.e. I want something]

In nonstandard English, of course, these sentences would have the same meaning, although in those dialects where negative concord is a variable feature its use may give additional emphasis to the negation of the second sentence.

5.2.1 Negative concord in Reading English

Although negative concord occurs in most nonstandard varieties of English, its syntactic distribution often varies. In the Black English

Vernacular, for example, there is an 'extraordinary proliferation of the negative' (see Labov, 1972d: 805), resulting in sentences such as this well-known example:

> It ain't no cat can't get in no coop (from *ibid.*: 773)

In Reading English the use of the negative is more restricted. Negative concord does not occur where there is a pre-verbal indeterminate: that is to say, sentences such as the above do not occur, nor do simpler constructions such as:

> Nobody couldn't come down here

Negative concord does, however, occur with post-verbal indeterminates, and also with the form *hardly*. Table 30 shows the frequency indices for negative concord with *any* and the *any*- compounds: it can be seen that it occurs very frequently in the boys' speech, but less frequently in the girls' speech. The number of tokens analysed was 141. Some examples follow:

1. *no < any* [determiner]: Oy, Hitler, you're gonna get your head bashed in. Not saying no names (Dave)
2. *none < any* [pronoun]: Give us that book, else I won't give you none, Alec (Smithy)
3. *nothing < anything*: You can know who he is, 'cos he's got one ear bitten away by leprosy, but the police don't do nothing about it (Debbie)
4. *no more < any more*: I can't remember her address no more, so I can't really ask her out (Ronny)
5. *no one < anyone*: You can come down here, mate, and talk to me, 'cos I won't have no one to talk to (Derek)
6. *nowhere < anywhere*: Well, I ain't been nowhere (Jeff)

Negative concord with *hardly* occurs very frequently in nonstandard varieties of English, and it is worth noting that some standard English speakers who never normally use nonstandard forms sometimes use *hardly* with a negative verb. In the peer group recordings *hardly* occurred only eight times; six of these occurrences showed negative concord, as in the examples below:

> The bloke can't hardly move, 'cos he gets raped by the girls every time he goes (Lynne)

> You're not hardly getting any (Rob)

The syntactic status of *hardly* is not at all clear. Like *scarcely, seldom* and *rarely, hardly* presents problems for analysis because it is a negative word with no obvious corresponding positive word, and it has been variously treated as an 'adverb of modality expressing negation' (Kruisinga and Erades, 1953: 89), a 'semi-negative' (Palmer, 1974: 28) and an inherently negative adverb (Wolfram, 1973: 152; Quirk et al., 1972: 380). Our data are unfortunately too limited to offer an empirical justification for any one analysis over another.

Table 30. *Frequency indices for negative concord with* any *and* any-*compounds*

	Orts Road boys	Shinfield boys	Shinfield girls
no < *any* [determiner]	90.00	(100.00)	80.00
none < *any* [pronoun]	77.78	–	40.00
nothing < *anything*	92.31	(66.67)	27.78
no more < *any more*	85.71	(100.00)	45.45
no one < *anyone*	(100.00)	–	(75.00)
nowhere < *anywhere*	(100.00)	–	(100.00)
Total	88.68	85.71	51.85

They can, however, provide some empirical support for Labov's analysis of *no* with a negated verb as related to the indeterminate *any*. In the peer group recordings *no* is used with uncountable nouns and with plural countable nouns, after a negated verb: it is used, in other words, as an equivalent form to standard English *any*:

> There wasn't no lights on (Nobby)
>
> That bloody stuff don't do no good anyway (Julie)
>
> . . . and I couldn't get no sleep (Mandy)

Nonstandard *no*, then, like standard *any*, is a negative alternative to *some*. With singular countable nouns the form *a* is used in both Reading English and standard English. *A* remains unchanged in negative sentences in both these varieties:

> He ain't got a prick (Nobby)
>
> Why didn't he give me a scrap down there, then? (Rob)
>
> I ain't got a light, Ed (Benny)

Negative concord, that is to say, cannot occur in this environment. This is illustrated very clearly in the sentence below:

It ain't got a Big Wheel, no Umbrellas (Debbie)

Debbie was talking here about the lack of amusements at a Hayling Island fairground. Negative concord does not occur with *a*: it does, however, occur within the next noun phrase, where the noun is plural and requires a negative indeterminate form.

The data do not, however, support Labov's analysis of *ever* as an indeterminate. His analysis is based on Klima's account of negation in English (Klima, 1964), and both these authors class *ever* as an indeterminate, along with *any* and *either*. For Labov, this may be due in part to the fact that in the Black English Vernacular negative concord apparently occurs with *ever* as well as with *any*, *any*- compounds and *either*. This is true of many British English dialects, also: the variety spoken in London is one example (see Labov, 1972d: 804). In Reading English, however, it seems that negative concord does not occur with *ever*. When peer group members use the negative form *never,* it is always with a non-negative verb:

I don't know. I've never been shagged (Tommy)

My mum's never had anybody die in our family (Ann)

Never is the only indeterminate in Reading English that does not undergo negative concord, and it is reasonable, therefore, to question its status as an indeterminate. There are, in fact, reasons for considering *never* as a temporal adverb rather than as an indeterminate (see Cheshire, 1981b), which would, of course, account for the fact that it does not enter into negative concord in Reading English.

Negative concord does, however, occur in Reading English with sentence modifiers, as in the example below:

No, that weren't my finger, neither! (Derek)

Sentence modifiers occurred only ten times in the recordings, and five of these showed negative concord. On each occasion the effect of negative concord was to reinforce the negative. Derek's sentence, for example, was the punch-line of a joke. Nobby's sentence, below, was emphatic in tone, with strong stress on the word *neither*:

Jeff: You don't look fifteen.
Nobby: Don't look it, don't act it, neither!

Where negative concord did not occur, sentences were not emphatic, but simply part of a continuing conversation. The stress in the following sentence, again from Nobby, fell this time on *clothes*:

Jeff: He don't go to discos, got no money –
Nobby: He ain't got no good clothes, either.

This clearly suggests that negative concord with a sentence modifier is an emphatic device that is available to speakers of Reading English, though not to speakers of standard English.

Negative concord differs from the other nonstandard features discussed here in that it has been extensively analysed elsewhere. Labov (1972d) presents a comprehensive account of negation in both standard English and nonstandard English which is based on two invariant rules of negative placement and negative attraction, and two variable rules of negative postposing and negative concord. Negation in Reading English would be adequately handled by these rules, provided only that *never* is not treated as an indeterminate.

5.3 *Never*

In standard English, *never* expresses the idea of 'universal temporal negation'. In other words, the meaning that *never* contributes to a sentence is 'not on any occasion', as the examples below illustrate:

She wears glasses, but she never puts them on (Debbie)

Shinfield never come down here, they're scared of us (Alec)

He never had stitches (Christine)

I never eats bogey's arse (Lynne)

5.3.1 *Never* as a negative preterite

In most nonstandard British English dialects, *never* also occurs with a more restricted meaning, that of 'not on one specific occasion':

And he hit my brother over the head, and he never even went down, and his head was pouring with blood (Nobby)

I never went to school today (Lynne)

I never said 'football', I said 'fall over' (Alec)

In these examples *never* corresponds to a negative preterite form. The standard English equivalents of these sentences, for example, would be:

> And he hit my brother on the head, and he didn't even go down . . .

> I didn't go to school today

> I didn't say 'football' . . .

Never as a negative preterite form can occur alone, like *didn't*. Compare, for example, these sentences:

> I bought the Pepsi (Debbie)

> You didn't. My mum bought it (Julie)

> I didn't, my mate did (Tommy)

> So they all went up and put them up, but I never (Nobby)

> I never, I never, it was him! (Dave)

The frequency of occurrence of nonstandard *never* is shown in Table 31, first when used alone, and then when used with a past tense verb form. The number of tokens was 146. The Table shows that the nonstandard preterite form is used more often, by all groups of speakers, when it stands alone in a sentence. This suggests that the use of *never* as a preterite form is an emphatic device used to reinforce a negative, for it occurs alone mainly in arguments, to contradict what has been said before. The exchange below is a good example:

> Tommy: Philly didn't use to hang about with us.
> Dave: He did.
> Tommy: Look, Philly *didn't* use to hang about with us.
> Dave: He did.
> Tommy: He never!

Table 31. *Frequency indices for nonstandard* never

Group	Alone	+ verb	All sentences
Orts Road boys	87.50	41.67	50.00
Shinfield boys	76.92	22.73	42.86
Shinfield girls	54.55	38.58	40.00
All speakers	71.88	35.90	43.62

5.3.2 Linguistic constraints on *never*

Only one linguistic constraint was found to affect the use of nonstandard *never*: this was a following complement. We saw earlier that the nature of a following complement affects the form of present tense verbs in Reading English in an interesting way: nonstandard verb forms occur less often when they are followed by a complement that is unmarked for tense, and less often still when they are followed by a complement that *is* marked for tense. Complements have an exactly similar effect on the form of the negative preterite: as Table 32 shows, the nonstandard preterite form occurs less often when it is followed by a complement where the verb is not marked for tense, as in the examples below:

> We didn't want to go to school (Mandy)
>
> She never knew how to lock it up (Nobby)
>
> I never let it roll backwards (Pete)

and it does not occur at all before complements where the verb *is* marked for tense:

> I didn't even know there was one missing (Tommy)
>
> . . . 'cos she didn't think it was my dog (Dave)
>
> And I didn't know my mum was there (Julie)

The constraint operates even when a complement is not actually uttered:

> I could ride a horse first time, and I didn't even know (Sharon)

This, then, is a very striking example of the regularity and consistency of variation in language. Not only is variation controlled by linguistic con-

Table 32. *Frequency indices for nonstandard* never *with following complements*

Group	+ complement (tense not marked)	+ complement (tense marked)	All sentences
Orts Road boys	(33.33)	(0.00)	50.00
Shinfield boys	(33.33)	0.00	42.86
Shinfield girls	0.00	0.00	40.00
All speakers	15.38	0.00	43.62

straints, but the same linguistic constraint can affect the occurrence of two quite distinct features of language. Both nonstandard *never* and present tense verbs are part of the verb phrase, of course, but *never* appears to function here in the same way as the 'empty' auxiliary DO, whereas those present tense verbs that are affected by the constraint are all lexical verbs; furthermore, *never* is negative, whereas nonstandard present tense verbs are not.

We can hypothesise that variation of such a systematic nature is connected to some general linguistic process; and probably this process has to do with linguistic change. We saw earlier (Section 4.1.6) that present tense verbs appear to be undergoing a change in the direction of standard English, and that the change seems to have been completed first in the environment of a following tense marked complement. *Never* may be undergoing a similar change. The form *never* as a past tense form is certainly found in earlier varieties of Berkshire English; *The Linguistic Atlas of England* (Orton et al., 1978), for example, shows *never done* as a form used in Berkshire for standard English *didn't do,* though, as we have seen, this survey does not provide data that are comparable with the present study. Maxim's older speakers use nonstandard *never* frequently, though they do not use negative preterite forms often enough for the occurrence of *never* in different linguistic environments to be analysed.

It seems possible, then, not only that language change spreads through one syntactic environment at a time, but that the same syntactic environment can affect a number of different changes; in this case, the nature of a following complement affects a preceding nonstandard negative past tense form, as well as a preceding present tense form. Clearly, however, more empirical research into the role of variation in morphological and syntactic change is needed in order to verify this hypothesis.

5.3.3 Syntactic status of *never*

The fact that *never* can apparently function unambiguously both as a universal temporal negator and as a negative preterite form has puzzled some writers (see, in particular, Labov, 1973a). Compare, for example, the scope of the negation in the following sentences, where *never* functions firstly as the universal temporal negator (in Lynne's sentence) and secondly as an apparent negative preterite (in Julie's sentence):

I've never won (Lynne) [i.e. on any occasion]

> I went out early, 'cos I never had nothing to do (Julie) [i.e. on one specific occasion]

Quirk et al. (1972: 376) class *never* as a time adverb. Although as an adverb it usually refers to universal time, it does occasionally occur in standard English with a more restricted meaning. With an adverb referring to future time, for example, *never* sometimes refers to a specific occasion:

> You will never catch the train tonight (from Quirk et al., 1972: 456)

Never is a 'negative minimizer' here, with the presence of the adverbial referring to future time (i.e. *tonight*) ruling out the temporal meaning of *never* (as Quirk et al. point out). In other words, *never* in this sentence means, quite simply, *not*. But because of its wider connotations elsewhere, as the universal negator, the negative element of the sentence is strongly emphasised (the meaning of the sentence being 'under no circumstances will you be able to get there in time'). It is, therefore, probably misleading to think of nonstandard *never* as a negative preterite form, even though it does appear to correspond to standard English *didn't*. It is used as a marker of negation, but whereas standard English uses the 'empty' auxiliary DO to carry the negative, nonstandard Reading English (in common with most other nonstandard British English varieties) makes more extensive use of the negative minimiser.

Where *never* occurs alone in a sentence it can be assumed to modify a deleted auxiliary *did*. In fact, the phrase *I never did* occurs frequently in some nonstandard varieties of English (though it does not occur in the peer group recordings).

The following exchange, for example, was recently overheard in London:

> We got let out of school early because the heating wasn't working.
> Out at half-past two! Well, I never did!

And the phrase *well I never* is a common feature of colloquial speech in both standard and nonstandard English.

6 *Relative pronouns*

6.1 Forms of the relative pronoun

There are five forms of the relative pronoun in standard English, and six in Reading English. The standard English forms are *who, whom, which, that* and zero, though *whom* is now used less often than before, especially in spoken English. In Reading English the form *what* is an additional possibility. With the exception of *whom,* these forms all occur in the peer group recordings:

> Every time I gave them a free kick which wasn't meant to be a free kick . . . (Nobby)
>
> You know the river that runs through there? (Alec)
>
> A girl I know went last week (Julie)
>
> Are you the little bastards what hit my son over the head? (Nobby)

The frequency of the different forms is shown in Table 33. The figures are based on 82 occurrences, all of which introduce restrictive clauses (there were only four nonrestrictive clauses in the recordings, all of which were introduced by a *wh-* form). The Table shows that the form that predominates varies according to whether it is the subject or the object of the relative clause, and whether the antecedent noun is personal or nonpersonal; and that in all cases it is a standard English form that predominates. When the relative pronoun is the subject, with a personal antecedent, the preferred form is *who*; when a subject pronoun has a nonpersonal antecedent the preferred form is *that.* The object pronoun occurs predominantly in the zero form, with both personal and nonpersonal antecedents.

The nonstandard form (*what*) occurs more often with a nonpersonal antecedent than with a personal antecedent, and it occurs most often when it has a nonpersonal antecedent and is the subject of the relative clause.

Table 33. *Frequency indices for relative pronoun forms*

Form	Personal subject	Personal object	Nonpersonal subject	Nonpersonal object
who	57.75	20.00	–	–
which	–	–	7.69	12.00
that	16.90	20.00	53.85	16.00
what	11.27	20.00	38.46	28.00
zero	14.08	40.00	0.00	44.00

6.2 Comparison with standard English forms

Quirk (1968) gives an analysis of forms of the relative pronoun in spoken standard English, which can serve as a useful comparison here. In restrictive clauses in his data *who* is the preferred form as a subject pronoun with personal antecedent, as it is in Reading English; as a subject pronoun with nonpersonal antecedent the form *which* is preferred, though *that* is a close second (see Quirk, 1968: 104). (*That*, as we have seen, is the preferred form in this environment in Reading English.) As an object pronoun with a personal antecedent, *wh-* forms, *that* and zero occur with almost equal frequency in Quirk's data, and with a nonpersonal antecedent *that* and zero occur more often than *which*.

As subject pronouns, then, there is little difference in the choice of relative pronouns in Reading English and standard English: both varieties prefer *who* when the antecedent noun is personal, and both varieties use *that* when the antecedent noun is nonpersonal, though standard English speakers use *which* slightly more often than *that*. The peer groups use *which* only rarely, preferring *that* or *what* (see Table 33).

As object pronouns, the differences are slightly more substantial. The peer groups prefer the zero form, with both personal and nonpersonal nouns; standard English speakers, however, do not use the zero form significantly more often than the other available forms with a personal antecedent, and they use *that* slightly more often than the zero form with a nonpersonal antecedent.

It is worth noting that use of the zero form is not restricted to object position in the peer group recordings, as it is in standard English (Quirk,

1968: 103). It does not occur after a nonpersonal antecedent (see Table 33), but it does occur after a personal antecedent:

> Owen Kelsey used to live next door to us has emigrated (Dave)
>
> Tell us the one about the lady couldn't get a lift (Jeff)

Use of the zero form, then, is more widespread in Reading English than it is in standard English. Reading English also has an additional form of the pronoun (*what*), as we have seen. In most cases, the peer group speakers appear to have a stronger preference than standard English speakers for one form over the others; but both varieties allow considerable variation in the form of the pronoun.

It should be noted also that relative clauses sometimes occur in Reading English where a simple pro-form would be used in standard English:

> I talks ever so different to what they do (Sue)

6.3 Linguistic constraints on forms of the pronoun

Quirk (1968) shows that in standard English the choice of relative pronoun is limited by other linguistic factors, such as the position of the pronoun relative to its antecedent, and the length of the relative clause. In the peer group recordings all relative pronouns except one immediately follow their antecedent noun, so that position cannot be considered as a potential constraint here. The choice of relative pronoun does, however, appear to vary systematically with clause length, as it does in standard English (Quirk, 1968: 107), though the difference in average clause length in the recordings is very small. Averages for object pronouns with nonpersonal antecedents show the zero clause as being 3.3 words, the *what* clause as 3.4, the *that* clause as 3.6 and the *who* or *which* clause as 3.9 (excluding the pronoun itself in all cases), compared to 4 words for a zero clause in Quirk's data, 5 for a *that* clause and 6 for a *which* clause (the *what* clause, of course, does not occur in standard English).

The distribution of forms in the peer group recordings suggests a lexical constraint, also, though occurrences are too few for this to be subjected to statistical tests of significance. Where *that* occurs in the preceding clause, whether as pro-form or as determiner, there appears to be a tendency for *that* to be used as the relative pronoun, with both personal and nonpersonal antecedents, and as both subject and object of the relative clause. *That* occurs 16 times in a preceding clause, and each time the relative pronoun is *that*:

That's one of the boys that gangs up on us (Marlene)

I like that record that's called Heartbreak Hotel (Julie)

Although *that* as a relative pronoun occurs in all the environments included in our analysis (i.e. as both subject and object, and with both personal and nonpersonal antecedents), it occurs most often (9 times out of 16) as a subject pronoun, with nonpersonal antecedent. It is perhaps worth noting that if these occurrences are excluded from the analysis, the nonstandard form *what* becomes the preferred form in this environment. *What* is used far more often than *which* in the peer group data (*which* occurs only 4 times out of a possible 38). This, of course, brings the relative pronouns into line with the interrogative pronouns, which have the personal form *who* and the nonpersonal form *what*. Interestingly enough, *what* also replaces *which* as the interrogative adjective in the recordings, with both personal and nonpersonal nouns:

What teacher do you like, then? (Ann)

What bit shall I give him? (Rob)

There is a general tendency, then, in the nonstandard variety, for *which* to be replaced by *what*; this results in a neat pattern of relative and interrogative forms, as Table 34 shows. The Table also shows the corresponding forms in standard English, for comparison.

Table 34. Who, what *and* which *in standard English and Reading English*

| | Standard English | | Reading English | |
	Personal form	Nonpersonal form	Personal form	Nonpersonal form
Relative pronoun	*who(m)*	*which*	*what*	*what*
Interrogative pronoun	*who*	*what*	*who*	*what*
Interrogative adjective	*which*	*which*	*what*	*what*

7 Other nonstandard forms

There are some remaining features that do not occur frequently enough in the peer group recordings to be analysed in detail, but that nevertheless have nonstandard forms of interest.

7.1 Prepositions

In both standard English and Reading English there are simple prepositions (consisting of one word, such as *in*, *up*) and complex prepositions (consisting of more than one word, such as *out of*, *except for*). However, some prepositional functions that are performed by a simple preposition in standard English are performed by a complex preposition in Reading English, and the reverse is also true.

For example, where standard English uses the simple preposition *off* to express direction away from an object (both literally and metaphorically) Reading English uses the complex preposition *off of*:

> She jumped off of the climbing frame (Mandy)
>
> And my mum, she's got about six weeks off of work (Debbie)
>
> But Sue's going off of her (Julie)

This difference in usage is functional, for it distinguishes *off of* from the simple preposition *off*, which sometimes occurs in Reading English where standard English would use *from*:

> Then I borrowed some stuff off my brother (Tommy)
>
> She always gets the money off my mum and dad (Nobby)
>
> I'll go and get a light off Al (Ed)

Conversely, the preposition *out*, which is usually followed by *of* in standard English to form a complex preposition, usually occurs alone in Reading English:

> They chucked him out their house (Nobby)

Table 35. *Prepositions in standard English and Reading English*

Standard English simple preposition	Standard English complex preposition	Reading English simple preposition	Reading English complex preposition
off			*off of*
from		*off*	
	out of	*out*	
to, at	*up to, up at*	*up*	
to, at	*down to, down at*	*down*	
to, at	*over to, over at*	*over*	
to, at	*round to, round at*	*round*	
on, zero		*round*	

He was leaning out the window (Rob)

Up, down and *over* are also used differently in Reading English:

We was smoking up his nan's, right (Nobby)

I lived one year down Staverton (Dave)

If you walks across this road, and over them bus stops . . . (Nobby)

She lives over Caversham (Rob)

In standard English a different preposition would be used (*to* or *at*); alternatively the same prepositions would be used with *to* or *at* to form a complex preposition (e.g. *up at his nan's*; *down at Staverton*; *over to the bus stops*). Thus when a complex preposition is reduced, the reduction in standard English is to its prepositional constituent, but in Reading English it is to its adverbial constituent. The adverbial constituents do not appear to relate systematically to direction on a vertical plane; speakers consistently use the phrases *up the station* and *down the hospital*, for example, though both the station and the hospital are in roughly the same area of the town (where the terrain is very flat).

Similarly, the preposition *round* occurs with no reference to circular movement, particularly after verbs like HIT and SLAP, where standard English would have either *on*, or no preposition at all:

She slapped her round the head (Julie)

She hit her round the face twice (Sue)

She went wham right round the fucking legs (Rob)

Frequency indices were not calculated for prepositions (with the exception of *off*, the nonstandard forms occurred 100 per cent of the time in the peer group recordings); the main differences, however, between prepositional usage in Reading English and standard English are summarised in Table 35.

7.2 Demonstratives

In both standard English and Reading English demonstratives are semantically marked for 'near' and 'distant' reference, as well as for number:

	Standard English		*Reading English*	
	Singular	*Plural*	*Singular*	*Plural*
'Near' reference	this	these	this	these
'Distant' reference	that	those	that	them

The use of the nonstandard form is clearest in the case of the determiner:

> If you walks across, there's a load of them bus stops (Nobby)

> I've seen them students, they're all scruffy (Smithy)

> 'Cos I was in between them two (Julie)

With the pronoun, it is often difficult to tell whether the nonstandard demonstrative or the standard plural personal pronoun is being used, since to a large extent the analysis depends on contextual and prosodic features. Debbie's sentence, below, illustrates this:

> I'd like one of them (Debbie)

If the articles in question are distant, then *them* is the nonstandard form; if they are near, then *them* is the standard form; the interpretation also depends on the stress that is given to the form. The distinction between near and distant reference is, of course, almost always linguistically redundant, since the point of reference is usually clearly apparent. The frequency of occurrence of the nonstandard form is very high in the boys' speech, but lower in the girls' speech, as Table 36 shows. Although χ^2 tests showed the figures to be significant, the Table is in fact based on only 19 occurrences of demonstrative pronouns. No linguistic constraints were found to affect the form of the demonstrative used by the peer groups.

The nonstandard form is very common in nonstandard British varieties of English, as well as in American English varieties (see Wolfram and Fasold, 1974: 175).

Table 36. *Frequency index for nonstandard* them

Group	Frequency index
Orts Road boys	91.67
Shinfield boys	100.00
Shinfield girls	33.33
All speakers	73.68

7.3 Reflexive pronouns

Reflexive pronouns were not often used by peer group members. There is some evidence, however, that the paradigm is more regular in Reading English than it is in standard English. In standard English two of the eight forms consist of the suffix *-self* (plural: *-selves*) added to the personal pronoun form (i.e. *himself*, *themselves*), whereas in the remaining forms the suffix is added to the possessive adjective (i.e. *myself*, *yourself*, *ourselves*, *yourselves*). In the nonstandard variety, however, it seems that the reflexive pronoun is formed in all cases by the addition of the suffix to the possessive adjective:

> Once he was scratching hisself and he'd caught it (Mandy)
>
> . . . and he had the Odeon to hisself (Julie)
>
> He was cross because one of his girls burnt theirself (Christine)

Furthermore, the suffix seems to be *-self* with plural pronouns as well as with singular pronouns, as Christine's sentence indicates (there were, in addition, four occurrences of the form *ourself*).

The first person reflexive form is usually *meself*:

> I looks after meself in the evenings (Nobby)

but this still maintains a regularly formed paradigm, since the possessive adjective usually has the form [mi:] in the data:

> Where's me fags gone? (Rob)

7.4 Nouns of measurement

Nouns of measurement are not marked for plurality in the recordings:

> From the road, it's about a thousand foot up (Derek)

It's not far away, really, it's only thirteen mile (Julie)

It's gonna cost us 37 pound for a few days (Lynne)

Plural marking is, of course, redundant here.

7.5 Adverbial constructions

7.5.1 Comparative adverbs

Comparative adverbs do not often occur in the recordings. The comparative form of the *bad–worse–worst* paradigm occurs three times: on one of these occasions the standard English form *worse* is used, but on the other two occasions a nonstandard form is used (a different nonstandard form each time):

No, she's badder (Julie)

It's usually worser than this (Tracy)

The form *worse* is also used where standard English would use *bad*:

Not as worse as these two stupid idiots (Ed)

Some other adverbs show 'double-comparison'. In standard English the comparative adverb is formed either by the addition of the suffix *-er*:

He thinks one foot is gonna grow bigger (Valerie)

or by the use of *more* plus the adverb:

He goes there more often than I do (Smithy)

Double-comparison uses both methods:

He's much more higher than me (Sharon)

Yes, but she gets more rougher (Mandy)

7.5.2 Non-distinction of adverbial and adjectival forms

In the recordings, some adverbials do not differ in form from the corresponding adjective:

We had it on fire one night, honest (Ed)

He writes really quick (Nobby)

I get on it easy (Derek)

I can't read that good (Ann)

There is also one example of an adverbial form used as an adjective:

> He done – sees this freshly dollop of shit (Derek)

However, this may have been a slip of the tongue: *done* may have been uttered too soon and, though corrected, not reintroduced after *freshly*.

7.6 'Intrusive' -*s*

An -*s* suffix occurs on a nominal in seven sentences in the recordings:

> Womens ain't allowed to look (Nobby)
>
> Yous has a slash at the toilet (Rob)
>
> Some peoples are going (Debbie)

An -*s* suffix also occurs on an adverb:

> And here they go nows (Jeff)

and on a preposition:

> Then he fucking runs off and leaves us all standing there (Rob)

There are too many occurrences for these to be explained as slips of the tongue. Possibly they are hypercorrect forms, connected with the non-standard present tense suffix (though hypercorrection would not be expected to occur in natural spontaneous speech of this kind).

PART III: SOCIOLINGUISTIC VARIATION

8 *Social variation*

8.1 Sociolinguistic analyses

It is an established fact that there are regular systematic patterns of sociolinguistic variation in English (see, for example, Labov, 1972b; Trudgill, 1978). These patterns can easily be discovered by analysing the language used by different groups of speakers; in this way it is possible to identify group norms that give social significance to specific linguistic features. By analysing the language of individual speakers, on the other hand, it is possible to show how speakers use the sociolinguistic system, perhaps unconsciously, to communicate their allegiance to specific social groups (see Le Page, 1968) or to express psychological states of mind (see Thakerar, Giles and Cheshire, 1982). The two approaches, group analysis and individual analysis, are complementary, and are best seen as reflecting different levels of abstraction, with group analysis at a more abstract level than individual analysis (see Romaine, 1980: 194). The primary approach, however, would seem to be the establishment of group norms, since little explanation of individual variation can be given without first establishing the social significance of the linguistic features. This chapter will begin, therefore, by establishing the broad patterns of sociolinguistic variation that emerge from a group analysis. Some of the variable linguistic features occur infrequently in the recordings, so they cannot be analysed sociolinguistically; but the majority of the features discussed in Part II will be considered.

8.2 Variation with sex of speaker

The members of the peer groups formed a homogeneous social group in that they were of similar ages and from similar social and regional backgrounds. They differed, however, in one important respect: 13 speakers were boys (the members of the Orts Road group and the

Shinfield boys group) and 11 speakers were girls (the members of the
Shinfield girls group).

Table 37 shows the frequency of occurrence of some of the nonstandard features in the speech of the boys and in the speech of the girls. With
the exception of the nonstandard past tense form *done* and the nonstandard present tense form *do*, the nonstandard forms are all used less often
by girls than by boys. In some cases the difference in frequency is very
small (as, for example, with present tense regular verbs and with nonstandard *has*); in most cases, however, the difference in frequency is more
substantial.

The categorical use of nonstandard *done* by both boys and girls maintains the earlier distinction made in this variety of English between full
verb DO (which has the past tense form *done*) and auxiliary DO (which
has the past tense form *did*). The distinction is much less rigidly maintained in the present tense forms of DO, as we have seen; and the fact that
boys use nonstandard *do* less often than the girls indicates that it could be
young male speakers who are leading the change towards the standard
English paradigm. Nonstandard *does*, on the other hand, like other
non-third singular suffixed present tense forms, is used less often by
girls.

Table 37. *Frequency indices for nonstandard features in the speech of
boys and girls*

Nonstandard feature	Boys	Girls
present tense -*s* (regular verbs)	53.16	52.04
present tense *has*	54.76	51.61
present tense *does* (full verb)	71.43	50.00
present tense 3rd singular *do* (auxiliary)	57.69	78.95
past tense *was*	88.15	73.58
past tense *were*	5.36	2.64
past tense *see*	85.71	44.44
past tense *come*	100.00	75.33
past tense *done*	100.00	100.00
ain't = auxiliary HAVE	92.00	64.58
ain't = copula BE	85.83	61.18
ain't = auxiliary BE	74.19	42.11
negative concord	88.33	51.85
never	46.84	40.00
relative pronoun	36.36	14.58
demonstrative adjective	92.31	33.33

Apart from these two exceptions, then, the nonstandard features are used more often by boys than by girls. This pattern of sex differentiation confirms the findings of many previous studies (see, for example, Labov, 1966; Wolfram, 1969; Trudgill, 1974). We should bear in mind, though, that whilst this approach is useful in revealing an overall pattern of sex differentiation, it may obscure the effect of other important social factors. In particular, it cannot reveal the way in which the linguistic features fulfil different social functions for the different sexes, as we will see.

8.3 Variation with peer group status

The peer groups differed not only in sexual composition but also in their internal structure. The boys' groups were more tightly structured than the girls' group; the Shinfield boys, for example, were very good friends and can be considered as forming a small, closely-knit peer group, as represented in Figure 2. The Orts Road group also contained a small, closely-knit group of four close friends; this can be considered as forming a central core within the group, as in Figure 3, though during the course of the recordings Derek gradually fell from favour with the younger boys. This fact is represented in Figure 3 by the broken line connecting Derek to the other members of the inner group. Rob and Nobby were special friends, as is shown by the double arrow. The single arrows in Figure 3 represent the direction of friendship: thus an arrow pointing in two directions indicates that friendship was mutual. Ronny and Benny, in the

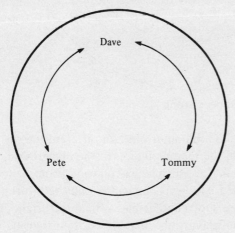

Figure 2   The Shinfield boys peer group

middle ring, were brothers, neither of whom formed close friendships with the inner group. Ronny was older than the other boys, and he no longer spent so much of his time with them. Although Benny was not much older than the boys in the inner group, he did not spend as much time as they did at the adventure playground; he said, in fact, that he spent most of his time in bed. Rick was popular with the rest of the group but, like Ronny, he was older than the other boys and no longer spent so much of his time with them. He had just left school and when the recordings began he was about to start work as a fork-lift truck operator.

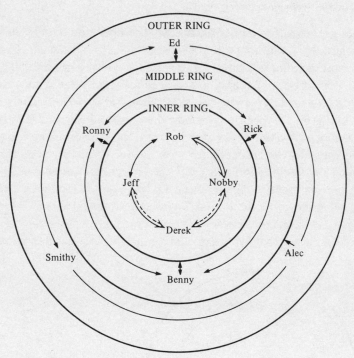

Figure 3   The Orts Road peer group

Ed, Alec and Smithy are all in the outer ring, for different reasons. At one time Ed had been one of the leading figures at the playground, and the boys still told stories of fights in which he had played a prominent part and of fires that he had started. However, he had now started work (as a trainee manager in a furniture shop) and he had a steady girlfriend, with the result that he visited the playground much less often than before. Smithy only came to the playground with Ed. The other boys made fun of him because he was not a good fighter, but they tolerated him because he was with Ed, and had apparently always been protected by Ed. Smithy did not like any of the other boys in the group; there is, therefore, no arrow linking his name to the rest of the group in Figure 3. Alec, similarly, did not appear to like any of the boys in the group, and he did not join in their games or other activities. His parents did not like him to go to the playground, and they even sent him to a different school to prevent his mixing with the local boys. This was difficult for him to avoid, however, since he lived in the public house next door to the playground, and he often joined in the other boys' jokes and conversations. He was usually teased by them, but they tolerated him, and he had apparently decided that the best way to avoid being bullied by his neighbours was to join them. The fact that he was merely tolerated by the group is shown in Figure 3 by a one-way arrow leading from Alec to the group.

A more rigorous description of the friendship patterns within the group can be obtained by means of a sociometric diagram, as in Figure 4. Following the procedure used by Labov in New York City (see Labov, 1973b), each speaker within the Orts Road group was asked to name the friends with whom he spent most of his time. The arrows represent the direction of naming. Solid lines show where reciprocal naming occurred, and represent the main social links within the group.

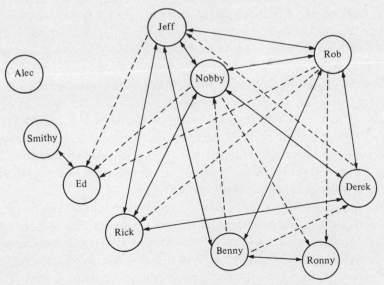

Figure 4   Reciprocal friendships within the Orts Road peer group

Table 38 shows the complete set of namings, with speakers classified into three groups. The classification is based on rather small differences in naming patterns, but it confirms the more impressionistic account of peer group structure given in Figure 3. The boys were asked to name their friends at a time when Derek was beginning to fall from favour; this is reflected in the naming patterns between Derek and the other boys, so he is classified here as a secondary member of the group rather than as a core member. The fact that Ed no longer considered himself part of the peer group can be seen from the fact that he did not name any boys except Smithy; but the effect of his former prestige is such that he was still named by several other group members. The peripheral status within the group of Smithy and Alec is also confirmed by the naming patterns in the Table.

We can now investigate the effect of peer group status on the use of nonstandard linguistic features. Table 39 shows the frequency of occurrence of nine of the most frequently occurring nonstandard features in the speech of core members, secondary members and non-members of the peer group. Six of the features are used more frequently by core members of the group, and four of these features (nonstandard present tense forms, *has*, *was* and *never*) show a regular decrease in frequency with peer group status.

There is some positive correlation, then, between the use of nonstandard features and peer group status. But the correlation does not hold for all the linguistic features, and it is much less regular and systematic than that found between the use of nonstandard features and peer group status in the New York study (see Labov, 1973b).

We can suggest two reasons for this. Firstly, one important finding that has emerged from studies of variation in British nonstandard English as opposed to the American Black English Vernacular is that different linguistic features often fulfil different social functions (see, for example, Romaine, forthcoming). Thus it is not atypical in a British context to find that some but not all of the nonstandard features of Reading English serve as markers of peer group status.

Secondly, although the Orts Road group is relatively cohesive in its structure, there are important differences between this and the peer groups studied by Labov. The Harlem groups had names (for example, 'the Jets', 'the Cobras'); they also had a distinctly hierarchical structure, with leaders and other 'officials'. These characteristics fulfil some of the criteria that have been said to define a 'gang' rather than a group (see

Table 38. *Naming patterns amongst members of the Orts Road group*

Speaker	Number of names given	Number of times named	Number of reciprocal namings
Core members			
Nobby	6	5	4
Jeff	5	5	4
Rob	7	4	4
Secondary members			
Derek	4	4	3
Ronny	1	3	1
Benny	5	3	3
Rick	3	4	3
Non-members			
Ed	1	4	1
Smithy	1	1	1
Alec	0	0	0

Downes, 1970: 149). The Orts Road group was less authoritarian and had a less rigid structure; these characteristics are typical of adolescent boys' street-corner groups in Britain (see, for example, Mays, 1954: 109; Willmott, 1966: 34), and may reflect the fact that the working classes are less socially isolated in Britain than they are in the U.S.A., so that there is less need for adolescents to identify with a group that is rigidly distinct from mainstream society. (To some extent the differences may also

Table 39. *Peer group status and frequency indices for nonstandard features*

Feature	Core members	Secondary members	Non-members
present tense -*s* (regular verbs)	68.39	42.33	30.38
present tense *has*	55.55	36.36	33.33
past tense *was*	90.32	86.49	60.00
past tense *were*	3.09	9.26	10.00
ain't = auxiliary HAVE	80.85	66.67	100.00
ain't = copula BE	92.31	77.77	86.36
ain't = auxiliary BE	64.86	75.00	100.00
negative concord	96.77	75.00	84.62
never	61.90	45.45	40.00

reflect differences between black and white culture – though Labov (1973b) deals with some white peer groups as well as with black groups.) It is worth noting, however, that the adventure playgrounds were used as special meeting places by both the Orts Road group and the Shinfield groups; and although the group members made no attempt to maintain the playgrounds as their own private territory (younger children also played there, for example), they sometimes had fights with groups from other parts of town who came to 'attack' their territory. On each of these occasions the individuals within the group formed a united front against the attackers, and when stories were later told about these fights the group members gave themselves a name – 'the Orts Road gang', or 'the Shinfield gang'. One fight had in fact taken place between these two groups, after a football match arranged by the playleaders. This behaviour corresponds to that of what has been termed 'near groups' – groups which lack persistence over time and any consensus on membership, but which act through the spontaneous mobilisation of individuals into a group in extreme situations, and which last only for the duration of the situation (Downes, 1970: 151).

The finding that the use of nonstandard linguistic features is not systematically correlated with peer group status, then, is in keeping with the flexible structure of adolescent peer groups in Britain, and confirms the fact that there is a very close interrelationship between language and social structure. In New York, where adolescent gangs are hierarchically structured and closely knit, there is a high correlation between the use of nonstandard features and peer group status. In Britain, where adolescent groups are more flexible in their structure, there is, correspondingly, a weaker correlation.

This is confirmed by the behaviour of the girls in this study. The Shinfield girls group was more loosely knit than the Shinfield boys group or the Orts Road group. All the girls knew each other, but as far as their main friendship patterns were concerned they fell into three separate sub-groups. Figure 5 shows the friendship patterns as they existed for most of the period of participant-observation. The numbers indicate the temporal order of friendships: unlike the boys, the girls tended to 'pair off', and each would have an intense though short-lived friendship with one other girl. Julie, for example, originally had Sue as what the girls termed her 'best friend'; she then transferred her affections to Shirley for a short time, and later to Debbie. At this point the rejected Sue and Shirley became 'best friends', and Julie became their sworn enemy.

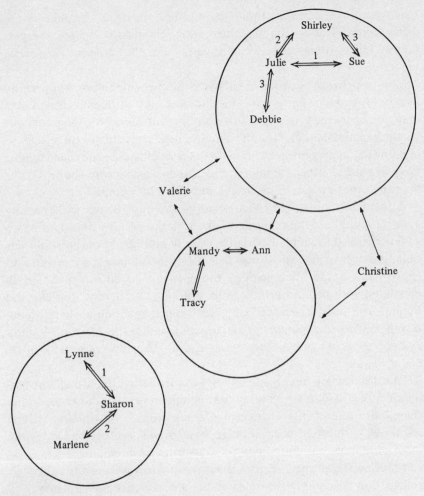

Figure 5   The Shinfield girls peer group

Sharon followed a similar pattern in her friendships, favouring first Lynne and then Marlene. Both Lynne and Marlene were outsiders to the group, though for different reasons. Lynne was thought to be too 'bad': she rarely went to school, she often stole from her parents and from shops, and she went 'too far' with her boyfriends. Marlene's behaviour tended towards the opposite extreme: she did not swear, she did not 'bunk' school or go out with boys, and she thought that she was socially superior to the other girls. Sharon's choice of outsiders as friends may have stemmed from the fact that her family had only recently been rehoused into the area, so that she had not yet been accepted by the main group of girls. But her fluctuating friendships echoed the pattern of Julie's friendships, which suggests that they followed a general tendency.

Mandy, in the third group of girls, was different in that she was friendly with both Ann and Tracy, though she was usually at the playground with only one of them. Christine, shown on the outside of the diagram, was younger than the other girls; she knew them all, but did not spend a lot of her time at the playground with them. Valerie did not spend much time at the playground either, though in this case it was because she was older than the other girls, and often out with her boyfriends.

A sociometric diagram constructed on the basis of the girls' naming patterns would not differ substantially from the pattern shown in Figure 5. When asked to name the friends with whom they spent most of their time, the girls named their 'best friends' of the moment; when asked to try to name some other people, the girls named all the other group members, with the exception of the 'outsiders' – Sharon, Marlene and Lynne. The double arrows in Figure 5 represent mutual 'best friend' namings. Christine named a friend at school as her 'best friend'; Valerie named Terry, her current boyfriend. The single arrows represent subsequent namings.

This distribution makes any attempt at correlating the use of nonstandard features with peer group status an impossible task, for there are no clear indications of differences in peer group status. Christine and Valerie stand out as different because their 'best friends' are not known by the other girls, but this alone does not constitute an adequate criterion for considering these two girls as a separate sub-group from the others. A comparison was attempted between the use of nonstandard features by Christine and Valerie and by each of the groups in the three circles in Figure 5 (Shirley was omitted, as she rarely featured in the recordings); not surprisingly, however, no systematic patterns of variation were found.

It seems, then, that in order to discover the social forces governing the use of the nonstandard features we need to look further than the composition of the peer groups.

8.4 The 'vernacular' and 'legitimate' sub-cultures

Peer group status in the New York groups is assumed to be linked to the use of nonstandard features by the norms of the vernacular culture. Labov (1973b: 83) describes the way in which these norms work:

> The overt norms of the dominant social class can operate to produce a consistent superordinate dialect . . . At the other end of the social spectrum, the covert norms of the street culture operate to produce the consistent vernacular of the urban working class.

The assumption is, then, that there are two opposing sets of norms that govern speech forms: overt norms, which govern the prestige standard English features; and covert norms, which govern the nonstandard vernacular forms. The fact that the use of nonstandard forms is governed by covert norms is neatly demonstrated in Trudgill's study (1972) of the English spoken in Norwich. Self-evaluation tests showed that most female speakers tended to over-report their use of certain standard phonological forms, presumably because of a desire to conform to the overt norms of society, which favour the prestige forms. Male speakers and younger female speakers, on the other hand, tended to under-report their use of these same features, in this case presumably because they were influenced by the covert norms, which favour the nonstandard forms.

The assumption that the norms of the vernacular culture are maintained and transmitted by the peer group provides an explanation for the fact that the use of nonstandard features is closely linked to peer group status in New York. In Britain, however, where peer groups are more informal in their structure, peer group status is not necessarily a relevant factor, as we have seen. British studies may require a different indicator of the extent to which behaviour is governed by vernacular norms, and it may be helpful, therefore, to consider in some detail the precise nature of these norms.

The vernacular culture should not be confused with the 'legitimate' teenage sub-culture that has grown up in Britain since the Second World War. This arose largely in response to the huge increase in the spending power of adolescents in the post-war years (Abrams (1959: 9) estimates that during the period 1945–50 the average real wage of teenagers increased at twice the adult rate), and is basically a consumer culture centring around clothes, fashion, films and music. The children who were involved in this study all participated in this 'legitimate' culture: the Shinfield girls were 'teeny-boppers', collecting photographs, posters and records of the current popular idols (at that time David Cassidy and Donny Osmond), while the Orts Road boys and the Shinfield boys spent their money on the mainstream 'glitter' singers (Gary Glitter and Alvin Stardust, for example) as well as on some of the more esoteric artists (such as David Bowie). These interests are considered part of the 'legitimate' teenage culture because mainstream society condones and encourages them as part of the mass consumer culture. The boys were also interested in football and played the game themselves as well as keenly following the progress of the teams that they supported; and they enjoyed other sports, including ferreting, pigeon-fancying, and swimming in the canal that ran alongside the playground. Again, these are all activities that can be accommodated within mainstream culture.

The children also took part in a number of more dubious exploits, however, which do *not* have the approval of mainstream society. Most of the children stole, both from shops and from their parents, though admittedly most of the thefts were petty. They also regularly set fire to the playground and to derelict houses, particularly in the Orts Road area, and they vandalised buildings and telephone boxes. Both boys and girls enjoyed fighting, and fights took place very frequently at the playgrounds, though the girls fought less often and less vigorously than the boys.

These activities were all sources of great prestige within the peer groups. The children who were good fighters, for example, were much admired, whilst those who were not so good were teased. Some of the children had been placed under supervision orders by local magistrates as a result of their 'delinquent' activities: Rick, for example, had been arrested after an incident at the Top Rank dance hall, where he had been tripping up girls on the dance floor and had attacked a bouncer who intervened; Derek and Benny had been summoned to the magistrates court because of persistent truancy, and Lynne for riding on horses 'borrowed' from a nearby paddock.

Delinquent behaviour of this kind is known to be typical of male working-class adolescent groups, and it has been described in several sociological studies (see, for example, Mays, 1954; Cohen, 1955; Andry, 1960; Downes, 1966). There has been shamefully little research to date into the behaviour of adolescent girls, though one study, at least, describes delinquent behaviour in a girls' group (see Smith, 1978). Most of the criminal offences involved are relatively trivial, and it seems that in the majority of cases delinquent behaviour is outgrown as the peer group is outgrown. Certainly the members of the Orts Road group and the Shinfield groups did not anticipate anything other than a conventional life for themselves: most of them expected to have a permanent job, to marry and have children – in short, to 'settle down'.

Adherence to the vernacular culture, then, should be seen as a temporary phase in the lives of the members of the peer groups. While they are involved in the culture, however, they are very strongly influenced by the norms and values that are inherent within it. Some of these can be seen as extensions of focal concerns of working-class culture: many of the boys' activities, for example, centre around what Miller (1958) calls the 'cultural foci' of 'trouble' (unlawful behaviour), 'excitement' (a way of avoiding boredom, often by taking risks), 'fate' (emphasising chance or luck), 'smartness' (in the American sense of 'outsmarting') and 'toughness'. Miller's cultural foci are derived from studies of working-class culture in the U.S.A., but a number of British studies confirm that these elements are characteristic of working-class life in Britain also (see, for example, Clarke, 1973; Willis, 1976).

8.4.1 The vernacular culture index

The boys' vernacular culture, then, is easy to define (partly because it is largely composed of activities that are known to be illegal). Since it is so clearly defined, it is possible to isolate a number of important elements that can be used as indicators in the construction of a 'vernacular culture index'. The use of a multiple-item index to measure the social characteristics of a sample is, of course, a standard sociological procedure. Its widest use has been in the measurement of socioeconomic class, but it is equally applicable to the measurement of other multi-dimensional social characteristics (see Finch and Hoehn, 1951). For example, a multiple-item index was used by Bhatnager (1970: 88–95) to measure the social adjustment of children from different racial backgrounds.

It seemed reasonable to assume that those aspects of the vernacular culture that were sources of prestige for the peer groups and that were frequent topics of conversation were of central importance within the culture. Six elements were selected on this basis.

One of the cultural foci mentioned earlier, 'toughness', was used as a sociological variable by Labov et al. (1968: 217–65) in a series of subjective reaction tests. One of the tests consisted of a single speaker reading sentences that differed mainly in the occurrence of a particular linguistic variable. Subjects were led to believe that the sentences were read by different speakers, and were asked to evaluate them on a number of scales, including a scale of 'toughness'. This involved answering the question 'If the speaker was in a street fight, how likely would he be to come out on top?' The 'toughness' scale was found to be positively correlated with the use of nonstandard linguistic features, in the judgements of subjects from all social classes. 'Toughness' was measured in a similar way (that is, by measuring *skill at fighting*) in the present study. As with other questions requiring an answer from all the participants, the necessary information was elicited from different speakers at different times during the period of participant-observation. At some point during the recordings, each boy was asked the questions 'Do you like fighting?' and 'Who do you reckon is a good fighter?'

Table 40 shows the answer given by each boy in the Orts Road group to the question 'Do you like fighting?', together with the number of times that he was named by the others as a good fighter. Only Benny, Alec and Smithy said that they did not enjoy fighting. Benny was renowned for starting fights by taunting other boys, and then retreating, leaving his friends to fight. Alec did not join in any of the group activities; and Smithy was not the fighting type, being small, thin and nervous. Their feelings about fighting are reflected in their ratings as fighters by the other boys. These three boys, then, were given a zero score for the indicator *skill at fighting*.

Rob and Derek were noncommittal when asked if they liked fighting: Rob said that he did when he was in the mood, and Derek just laughed. Again, their feelings are reflected in their ratings: only three boys thought that Rob was a good fighter (these were Benny, Alec and Smithy!) and four thought that Derek was a good fighter. Only four boys rated Jeff as a good fighter, though he said that he enjoyed fighting. Rob, Derek and Jeff were each given a score of 1 for this aspect of their behaviour.

Nobby, Rick, Ronny and Ed all had high ratings, and all said that they liked to fight; these boys were each given a score of 2.

The three Shinfield boys, Dave, Peter and Tommy, were also given a score of 2. They said that they liked to fight, and they named each other as good fighters, in addition to some other boys who did not take part in the study.

Fighting, of course, involves elements other than 'toughness': 'violence', 'excitement', and possibly 'chance' are all involved. These aspects of the culture are also bound up with the second and third indicators of adherence to the vernacular culture: *carrying of weapons* and participation in minor *criminal activities* (arson, vandalism and shop-

Table 40. *Skill at fighting*

Speaker	'Do you like fighting?'	Number of times named as a good fighter
Rick	yes	8
Nobby	yes	7
Ed	yes	7
Ronny	yes	6
Jeff	yes	4
Derek	?	4
Rob	?	3
Benny	no	0
Alec	no	0
Smithy	no	0

lifting). Though interrelated, these are treated as separate indicators because not all boys took part in all these activities to the same extent.

Although a great deal of prestige was associated with the carrying of weapons, not many of the boys actually did so. Nobby had a knife, and Rick a chain, and stories were often told of fights where they had been used. Dave and Pete also carried knives and said that they used them in fights. Tommy did not have any kind of weapon, saying that he could rely on his fists. If the other boys had not laughed, this might have been taken as an indication that he was exceptionally tough. Since they did laugh, however, only Nobby, Rick, Dave and Pete were given a score of 1 for the feature *carrying of weapons*.

Only five boys said that they never took part in any criminal activities. Two had apparently only recently reformed: Ed, as we have seen, had changed his behaviour considerably since he had started work, and Derek was looking forward to leaving school and joining the Army, and had apparently reformed in anticipation of his Army career. (This may, of course, explain why he fell from popularity with core members of the peer group.) Benny, Alec and Smithy had never taken part in any criminal adventures. These five boys, then, were given a zero score for the indicator *criminal activities*, and the remaining boys were given a score of 1. At first the boys were scored separately for shoplifting, arson and damaging property, but this was found unnecessary since any boy who indulged in one of these activities also indulged in the others.

Many of the playground conversations centred around what the boys would do when they left school. Rick, Ed and Smithy had in fact already left school and were employed respectively as a fork-lift truck operator, a trainee shop manager and a shop assistant. Ronny had also left school, but was unemployed. The other boys clearly admired Rick's choice of occupation, and asked him questions about the truck and about the building site where he worked. They were very scathing, however, about Ed's and Smithy's jobs, and also about Ronny, making jokes, mostly behind their backs, about shop life and about life 'on the dole', and occasionally teasing them to their faces. Those boys who were still at school had many discussions about their future jobs. Alec, who had decided to enter the Civil Service as a clerical assistant, was unmercifully teased, and so was Benny, who said he wanted to do nothing. Jobs that the group considered acceptable seemed to carry connotations of masculinity and aggression, and to reflect once more the cultural norms of 'trouble' and 'excitement'. Nobby, for example, wanted to be a slaughterer, like his father, because he wanted 'to kill animals'. The other boys' choices of jockey, train driver, soldier, lorry driver and motor mechanic also met with group approval.

Table 41 shows the jobs that the boys wanted to have or, in the first four cases, the jobs that they already had (or did not have, in Ronny's case). Those boys who had chosen jobs that met with group approval were given a score of 1 for the indicator *jobs*, as Table 41 shows; the other boys were given a zero score.

Two further indicators were chosen on the grounds that they were of symbolic importance within the groups. Many writers have stressed the importance of *style* as a symbolic value within adolescent sub-cultures, and for six of the boys dress and hairstyle were frequent topics of conversation and important aspects of their self-esteem. Their preferred dress was Levi jeans, closely-fitting sweaters and boots with high soles and heels, and their hair was worn short. The other boys did not show any interest in clothes, with the exception of Ed, who said he nowadays liked to 'look smart' in a shirt and suit. Benny, for example, always wore plimsolls, and was often teased about this.

This preoccupation with clothes could, of course, anticipate a future involvement with the 'legitimate' teenage consumer culture, where large amounts of time and money are spent on personal appearance. At present, however, the boys did not have enough money to be too preoccupied with clothes. And in any event, their preferred style suggests that they were identifying not with the 'legitimate' culture but with the 'illegitimate' skinhead sub-culture, which involved ostentatiously 'dressing

Table 41. *Jobs*

Speaker	Job	Score
Rick	fork-lift truck operator	1
Ed	trainee shop manager	0
Smithy	shop assistant	0
Ronny	out of work	0
Nobby	slaughterer	1
Jeff	jockey	1
Rob	train driver	1
Benny	hoped to be out of work	0
Derek	soldier	1
Alec	clerk	0
Tommy	lorry driver	1
Pete	motor mechanic	1
Dave	soldier	1

down' in order to disassociate themselves publicly from those who were preoccupied with current fashion (see Cohen, 1976: 46; Hebdige, 1979: 55).

Those boys for whom *style* was important, then, were given a score of 1; the other boys were given a zero score.

Finally, a measure of *swearing* was included in the index, since this was a major symbol of vernacular identity for both boys and girls. All the boys except Alec and Smithy swore very frequently indeed at the playgrounds, though some of them said that they did not swear at home or at school. Swearing was often discussed, and those who did swear seemed to view it as an act of bravado. It seemed significant that Alec and Smithy, who scored zero on all the other indicators, said *f— off* and *b—* rather than *fuck off* and *bloody*, as the other boys did. *Swearing* is, of course, a linguistic feature, but this does not affect its use as an indicator since it involves only a few lexical items which do not occur in a relevant variable form. Alec and Smithy, then, scored zero for this feature, and the other boys were given a score of 1.

The behaviour of the boys with regard to each of the indicators discussed above can be summarised on a Guttman scale, as in Table 42. Those boys whose behaviour conformed to the vernacular norm were given a plus on the scale, and those boys whose behaviour did not conform to the norm were given a minus. *Skill at fighting*, which had been shown by a three-valued score, was reduced to a two-valued score for the purposes of the scale: boys

Table 42. *Guttman scale for elements of vernacular culture*

Name	Carrying of weapons	Style	Jobs	Criminal activities	Skill at fighting	Swearing
Nobby	+	+	+	+	+	+
Dave	+	+	+	+	+	+
Pete	+	+	+	+	+	+
Tommy	−	+	+	+	+	+
Rob	−	+	+	+	+	+
Jeff	−	+	+	+	+	+
Rick	(+)	−	+	+	+	+
Ronny	−	−	−	+	+	+
Derek	−	−	(+)	−	+	+
Ed	−	−	−	−	+	+
Benny	−	−	−	−	−	+
Alec	−	−	−	−	−	−
Smithy	−	−	−	−	−	−

who had received a score of 1 or 2 were given a plus on the scale, whilst boys who had received a zero score were given a minus.

The two entries in parentheses do not fit the otherwise regular pattern of variation. In spite of this, the coefficient of reproducibility is 0.97, a figure which shows that the data can be regarded as scaleable (see Pelto, 1970: Appendix B).

The scores that each boy obtained for each of the indicators are shown in Table 43. Individual totals represent the vernacular culture index of each of the boys: that is, they provide a measure of the extent to which they adhere to the vernacular culture. The boys can now be classified into four groups on the basis of their total scores, with boys who adhere most closely to the norms of the vernacular culture in Group 1, and boys who adhere least closely in Group 4:

> Group 1: Nobby, Dave, Pete
> Group 2: Rick, Tommy, Jeff, Rob, Ronny
> Group 3: Derek, Ed, Benny
> Group 4: Alec, Smithy

8.4.2 Linguistic markers of adherence to the vernacular culture

Eleven of the variable linguistic features occur frequently enough in the playground conversations to allow analysis of the extent to which they

Table 43. *Vernacular culture index*

Indicator	Nobby	Dave	Pete	Rick	Tommy	Jeff	Rob	Ronny	Derek	Ed	Benny	Alec	Smithy
Carrying of weapons	1	1	1	1	0	0	0	0	0	0	0	0	0
Style	1	1	1	0	1	1	1	0	0	0	0	0	0
Jobs	1	1	1	1	1	1	1	0	1	0	0	0	0
Criminal activities	1	1	1	1	1	1	1	1	0	0	0	0	0
Skill at fighting	2	2	2	2	2	1	1	2	1	2	0	0	0
Swearing	1	1	1	1	1	1	1	1	1	1	1	0	0
Total score	7	7	7	6	6	5	5	4	3	3	1	0	0

mark adherence to the vernacular culture. Table 44 shows the frequency with which the nonstandard forms are used by each of the four groups of boys. As before, bracketed figures indicate that the number of occurrences is low. Figures for the nonstandard -s suffix, *ain't* and nonstandard *never* are adjusted to take into account the effect of the linguistic constraints governing the occurrence of these nonstandard forms.

Table 44. *Adherence to vernacular culture and frequency indices for nonstandard features*

Feature	Group 1	Group 2	Group 3	Group 4
Class A				
nonstandard -s	77.36	54.03	36.57	21.21
nonstandard *has*	66.67	50.00	41.65	(33.33)
nonstandard *was*	90.32	89.74	83.33	75.00
negative concord	100.00	85.71	83.33	71.43
Class B				
nonstandard *never*	64.71	41.67	45.45	37.50
nonstandard *what*	92.31	7.69	33.33	0.00
Class C				
nonstandard *do*	58.33	37.50	83.33	–
nonstandard *come*	100.00	100.00	100.00	(100.00)
ain't = auxiliary HAVE	78.26	64.52	80.00	(100.00)
ain't = copula BE	100.00	76.19	56.52	75.00
ain't = auxiliary BE	58.82	72.22	80.00	(100.00)

The features are arranged into three classes in the Table, on the basis of the extent to which they reflect adherence to the vernacular culture. Class A consists of features whose frequency is very finely linked to the boys' vernacular culture index. The most sensitive indicator of adherence to the vernacular culture is the nonstandard present tense suffix, which is used very frequently by Group 1 speakers, progressively less frequently by speakers in the other groups and rather infrequently by speakers in Group 4. The other features in Class A also show a positive correlation with the vernacular culture index, though the differences in frequency are not so great.

The two features in Class B show significant variation only between Group 1 speakers and Group 4 speakers: in other words, between those boys who adhere most closely to the vernacular culture and those boys who adhere least closely. This type of sociolinguistic variation is not unusual; Policansky (1980), for example, reports on a similar pattern of variation for subject-verb concord in Belfast English between speakers at the extreme ends of a social network scale. In fact, when Groups 2 and 3 are combined, a regular pattern of variation does emerge, as Table 45 shows. These features, then, do mark adherence to the vernacular culture, but they are less sensitive markers than the features in Class A, showing regular patterning only with broad groupings of speakers.

Table 45. *Frequency indices for Class B features*

Feature	Group 1	Groups 2 & 3	Group 4
nonstandard *never*	64.71	43.00	37.50
nonstandard *what*	92.31	18.00	0.00

Use of the features in Class C, on the other hand, is not correlated with adherence to the vernacular culture. The nonstandard past tense form *come* is used categorically by *all* speakers irrespective of their vernacular culture index (this echoes the distribution of the past tense form *done*, which is also used categorically by all speakers – see Section 4.2.2). Nonstandard *do* and *ain't* have an erratic distribution, and it tends to remain this way even when the boys in Groups 2 and 3 are amalgamated into a single group, as Table 46 shows. Nonstandard *do* now shows a minimal decrease in its use by Group 1 speakers and Group 2 speakers; but the distribution of *ain't* remains completely irregular.

We can conclude, then, that these three features do not mark adherence to the vernacular culture. Nonstandard *come* is apparently an

Table 46. *Frequency indices for Class C features*

Feature	Group 1	Groups 2 & 3	Group 4
nonstandard *do*	58.33	57.00	–
nonstandard *come*	100.00	100.00	(100.00)
ain't = auxiliary HAVE	78.26	70.00	(100.00)
ain't = copula BE	100.00	65.91	75.00
ain't = auxiliary BE	58.82	75.00	(100.00)

invariant dialect feature for boys; nonstandard *do* and *ain't* are variable features, but variation does not fulfil the same social function here as it does elsewhere. Nonstandard *never* and nonstandard *what* function only loosely as markers of the vernacular culture. The remaining features, however – nonstandard *-s*, *has*, *was* and negative concord – are sensitive markers of the extent to which boys belong to the vernacular culture. This is particularly true of the nonstandard present tense suffix.

8.5 Vernacular culture and its effect on girls

The girls took part in the same kind of 'delinquent' activities as the boys: they set fire to the playground from time to time, and they stole from shops and from their mothers' purses. Lynne, as we have seen, had been placed under a supervision order for 'borrowing' horses, and Valerie, together with her boyfriend and his friend, had stolen a car.

However, the girls had a different attitude towards these activities. They did not boast about their exploits, as the boys did, and they did not seem to be accorded any prestige for them by their friends. Although, like the boys, they took part in fights, the fights occurred only as extensions of arguments, and never as events in their own right. Furthermore, the girls did not tell stories of past fights or pick out particular girls as good fighters. Thus the girls' participation did not seem to reflect any deep-rooted cultural involvement; they did not appear to attach any particular value, for example, to the norms of 'toughness', 'excitement' and 'violence'.

This meant that it was difficult to define the value system of the girls' group. In some ways the girls adhered more closely to the values of the mainstream consumer culture, for their principal interests lay in pop music, films, television, and boyfriends. This does not mean, though, that they conformed generally to the values of mainstream society, for most of them hated school, were contemptuous of their teachers, and sneered at girls who went to private schools, at university students, and at anyone who spoke with a 'posh' accent.

One reason for the difficulty of defining the girls' cultural values is that they did not spend so much time at the adventure playground as the boys did, and they were noncommittal about what they did when they were not there. The older girls did not often visit the playground, spending some of their time with other girls, at home, and some with their boyfriends. The younger girls used the playground as a meeting place, but they still spent a lot of their time at home. This was partly because they were expected to help with household chores and with the care of their younger brothers and sisters, whereas the boys were sent outdoors, but it was also because they visited each other at home more often than the boys did, to listen to records and to experiment with make-up and clothes. This appears to confirm the theory that working-class girls interact amongst themselves within the 'culture of the bedroom' to form a teenage consumer culture that is distinct from boys' sub-cultures. Boys' sub-cultures tend to be oriented away from the home, leading boys into the streets and to their 'mates'; girls' interests, on the other hand, often remain focused on the home and on their eventual marriage (see McRobbie and Garber, 1976: 213). The reasons for this must stem largely from the different ways in which boys and girls are treated by their parents and by society during childhood; and this may explain why the boys' peer groups in this study are more cohesively structured than the Shinfield girls' group. The Orts Road group, for example, had a central 'core' of four boys, but at the playground these boys chatted and 'messed around' with anyone else who was there. The girls, on the other hand, chatted and played in small groups, ignoring other girls who were at the playground; and, as we have seen, they followed a pattern of fluctuating individual friendships that excluded previous friends. This behaviour confirms a previous description of the behaviour of adolescents:

> . . . as they grow towards adolescence, girls do not need groups; as a matter of fact for many of the things they do, more than two would be an obstacle . . . Boys are dependent on masculine solidarity within a relatively large group. In boys' groups the emphasis is on masculine unity; in girls' cliques the purpose is to shut out other girls. (Henry, 1963: 131–2)

Since the girls did not belong to a closely-knit group and did not have a clearly defined system of cultural values, it was not possible to measure their vernacular loyalty by means of a vernacular culture index. It *was* possible, however, to make a broad division between the girls who showed some degree of adherence to a culture other than the mass 'legitimate' teenage culture (the majority of the Shinfield group) and the three girls who did not. Sharon, Christine and Marlene were different from the other girls in that they did not swear, steal or set fire to the playground, and they did not play truant from school. They said that the other girls were 'rough' and 'common', and they had been told by their parents to stay away from the playground – though they did not in fact do so.

Table 47 compares the frequency with which some of the nonstandard linguistic features occur in the speech of the three 'good' girls and the rest of the Shinfield girls. This division is, of course, far from ideal, since we are comparing a group of three speakers with a group of nine, but it does give some indication of the way in which the linguistic features function as markers of vernacular loyalty for the girls.

Table 47. *Frequency indices for non-standard features in the speech of 'good' and 'bad' girls*

Feature	'Good' girls	'Bad' girls
nonstandard -*s*	25.84	57.27
nonstandard *has*	36.36	35.85
nonstandard *was*	63.64	80.95
negative concord	12.50	58.70
nonstandard *never*	45.45	41.07
nonstandard *what*	33.33	5.56
nonstandard *come*	30.77	90.63
ain't = copula	14.29	67.12

The Table shows that five features are used less often by the 'good' girls than by the others: the nonstandard -*s* suffix, *was*, negative concord, nonstandard *come* and *ain't* (as copula – there were too few occurrences of *ain't* as auxiliary for this to be included). Three of these function as markers of vernacular loyalty for boys also, as we have seen – nonstandard -*s*, *was* and negative concord. Nonstandard *come*, however, does not function in this way for boys; for them it is an invariant feature, used categorically by all speakers. The 'bad' girls use this feature almost categorically (90.63 per cent of the time); but the 'good' girls use it relatively infrequently (only 30.77 per cent of the time), preferring the standard English form *came*. There is an interesting pattern of sex differentiation here, then: *come* is a marker of vernacular loyalty for girls, but not for boys.

This appears to be the case for *ain't*, too: the 'good' girls use this form considerably less often than the other girls, whereas there are no systematic differences in its use by the different groups of boys.

A further difference between girls and boys lies in the function of the nonstandard form *has*. This is a marker of vernacular loyalty for boys, showing systematic variation with the extent to which they adhere to the norms of the vernacular culture. For girls, however, the form does not function in this way, for there is virtually no difference between the use of *has* by 'good' girls and its use by 'bad' girls.

Nonstandard *never* and *what* functioned only loosely as vernacular markers for boys. For girls, they do not appear to function in this way at all: in fact, the 'good' girls use these nonstandard forms more often than the other girls.

The fact that linguistic features can sometimes serve as markers of vernacular loyalty for girls but not for boys, and vice versa, has important consequences for the analysis of sex differentiation in speech. We saw earlier that a straightforward analysis of sex differentiation found that girls use the five features listed in Table 48, for example, less often than boys – a result which substantiates previous findings and which apparently confirms that girls are more susceptible to the overt norms that control use of the prestige standard English forms. The left-hand side of Table 48 shows the figures that result from this kind of analysis. In fact, however, these figures obscure the real nature of sex differentiation. The right-hand side of the Table shows the way in which these features are used by girls and boys who share the same degree of adherence to the vernacular culture – the three 'good' girls and the two 'good' boys who scored zero on the vernacular culture index. We can see that although the difference in the frequency of use of nonstandard -*s* remains small, it is in fact the *boys* who now seem more susceptible to the overt norms controlling the use of standard English forms, for the boys use the nonstandard forms less often than the girls. The patterns of variation for nonstandard *was*, on the other hand, remain virtually unchanged: 'good' girls use the nonstandard form

Table 48. *Frequency indices for nonstandard features in the speech of all boys and girls and of 'good' boys and girls*

Feature	All boys	All girls	Difference	'Good' boys	'Good' girls	Difference
nonstandard -*s*	53.16	52.04	−1.12	21.21	25.84	+4.63
nonstandard *was*	88.15	73.58	−14.42	75.00	63.64	−11.36
negative concord	88.33	51.85	−36.48	71.43	12.50	−58.43
nonstandard *come*	100.00	75.33	−24.67	(100.00)	30.77	−69.23
ain't = copula	85.83	61.18	−24.65	75.00	14.29	−60.71

less often than 'good' boys, and the difference in frequency is of approximately the same order as it is on the left-hand side of the Table. The
other features – negative concord, nonstandard *come* and *ain't* – are all
used much less often by girls than was indicated by the conventional
analysis, as can be seen from the figures in the 'Difference' column on the
far right.

The main point that emerges from this analysis, then, is not that girls
are more susceptible to the overt norms governing the use of standard
English features (though this is certainly *to some extent* true), but that
different linguistic features are used in different ways by boys and girls.
Thus negative concord, nonstandard *come* and *ain't* can be considered as
sex markers: they are used very much more often by boys than they are by
girls. Even the 'good' boys use these nonstandard forms more than 70 per
cent of the time; by comparison, they are used very infrequently by the
'good' girls. Nonstandard *was* does not function as a significant sex
marker; and nonstandard *-s* does not function as a sex marker at all.

The figures in Table 49 confirm this analysis. The columns headed
'Boys' show the frequency with which boys who show some adherence to
the vernacular culture use the nonstandard features (as we have seen, the
boys in Group 1 adhere most closely to vernacular norms, and the boys in
Groups 2 and 3 progressively less closely), and the far right-hand column
shows the frequency with which girls who show some adherence to
vernacular norms use these features. Nonstandard *-s*, which is not a sex
marker, does not show any significant difference in use by boys and girls:
the 'bad' girls use the nonstandard form with approximately the same
frequency as the boys in Group 2. Nonstandard *was* shows a progressive,
though small, decrease in frequency between Group 1 boys and Group 3
boys, and a similar decrease between Group 3 boys and 'bad' girls. There
is *some* correlation with sex here, then, but not enough for *was* to be
considered a true sex marker. Negative concord, on the other hand, is
used significantly less often by 'bad' girls than it is by any of the boys'
groups, and nonstandard *come* is also used less often by the 'bad' girls;
this confirms, then, that these features *are* sex markers. *Ain't* is more
irregular in its distribution: the 'bad' girls use it less often than the boys in
Groups 1 and 2, but more often than the boys in Group 3. The reason
could lie in the fact that *ain't* functions as a marker of vernacular loyalty
for girls, as we have seen; although a dual function seems to be perfectly
possible for some features (negative concord, for example, functions as a
sex marker and also as a marker of vernacular loyalty for both boys and

Table 49. *Frequency indices for nonstandard features in the speech of 'bad' boys and girls*

Feature	Group 1	Boys Group 2	Group 3	'Bad' girls
nonstandard -*s*	77.36	54.03	36.57	57.27
nonstandard *was*	90.32	89.74	83.33	80.95
negative concord	100.00	85.71	83.33	58.70
nonstandard *come*	100.00	100.00	100.00	90.63
ain't = copula	100.00	76.19	56.52	67.12

girls), for other features, such as *ain't*, one function appears to take precedence over another, so that its principal social function is the marking of vernacular loyalty in girls' speech. The fact that it marks vernacular loyalty only for girls, of course, means that *ain't is* a sex marker, though the marking is at a more abstract level here. The reason may also be connected with the fact that *ain't* can function as an overt marker of a vernacular norm, as we saw in Section 5.1.5.

This analysis confirms Milroy's findings (1980) that different linguistic features fulfil different social functions. Some features of nonstandard Reading English function as markers of vernacular loyalty for girls, for boys, or for both girls and boys. Others function as sex markers; and some function as both.

9 *Stylistic variation*

9.1 Constraints on speech style

Most of the features of Reading English occur variably, alternating in occurrence with the corresponding standard English forms. This study has focused so far on the variation that occurs in the informal speech used in natural spontaneous conversations. Previous studies have shown that in more formal situations (such as in interviews, or when reading aloud) speakers tend to use an increased proportion of standard English forms, and it has been assumed that this is because they are, perhaps unconsciously, paying more attention to the way that they speak. Labov (1972b: 99) suggests that speech style can be seen as a linear continuum ranging from informal style to formal style and corresponding to the amount of attention that is given to speech. He assumes that all speakers within a speech community share the same overt evaluative norms, so that when they concentrate on the way that they speak they tend to use more of the prestigious standard speech forms. In fact, however, speech style is more complex than this. In some cases the result of paying more attention to speech is an increased use of *nonstandard* forms – perhaps in order to produce an informal style appropriate to the occasion (see Wolfson, 1976: 203), or to use a style that 'converges' towards the speech of a person to whom one is well disposed (see Giles and Smith, 1979). There are many factors that can affect speech style: the degree of intimacy that exists between speakers, for example, and their relative status, the setting of the speech event, and the topic of conversation; and we can assume that there are other relevant factors that have not yet been defined. The ways in which individual speakers respond to these constraints may vary, and this suggests that speech style can best be seen as the way in which speakers respond to a given situation. The most 'natural' speech style occurs in spontaneous everyday interactions, as we have seen; in other situations speakers modify the way that they speak to produce the style that they consider appropriate for the occasion.

This chapter will analyse the ways in which the peer group members modify their speech when they are in a situation that is different from the relaxed, easy-going environment of the adventure playground.

9.2 The school recordings

The school is an environment that provides a particularly interesting comparison. The school, as an established social institution, inevitably embodies the values of the dominant culture in society (see Moss, 1973: 42–3), and this means that those children who adhere most closely to the norms of the vernacular culture will inevitably experience some degree of cultural conflict when they are at school. This, of course, partly explains why they 'bunk' school so often. Unfortunately the fact that the children did not attend school regularly meant that it was difficult to obtain adequate data for a linguistic analysis of 'school style'. Lynne, for example, had recently been referred by her headmaster to a centre for chronic truants, and it was not possible, therefore, to record her in school. Most of the other girls behaved so badly when they were at school that they were very unpopular with their teachers – so much so that the teachers were unwilling to single them out for special attention by making tape recordings of them.

Four boys – Ed, Rick, Ronny and Smithy – had left school. Alec also left whilst the recordings at the adventure playground were in progress. None of these speakers, therefore, could be included in the analysis of stylistic variation. Secondary school allocation in Reading at that time was based on a system of parental choice, and the children in this study who were still at school attended a total of eight different schools. Their schools were contacted after the recordings in the adventure playground had been completed, and their class-teachers were asked to record them with two or three friends, and the teacher, in the classroom. (Some extracts from these recordings were given in Part I.) I deliberately took no part in any of the school recordings.

Only three of the girls' teachers could be persuaded to take part in the study; the rest refused on the grounds that the girls in question were rarely at school. One teacher was extremely reluctant to record her 'four worst trouble-makers', but eventually made a short recording of them in their drama group. This was not what had been required, and the recording was short and far from adequate. Ann's teacher was more co-operative, but in spite of the presence of her school friends Ann was overawed by the situation and could scarcely be persuaded to utter a word. Sharon's and Marlene's teacher was the only one who was happy to provide a tape recording – not surprisingly, perhaps, since these were 'good' girls who behaved relatively well at school. Data on style-shifting, then, exists for seven of the Shinfield girls – Julie, Debbie, Sue, Mandy, Ann, Sharon and Marlene – though in very limited quantities.

The boys' teachers, on the other hand, appeared to like the boys they were asked to record, despite the fact that these boys behaved badly at school. This is an interesting contrast, perhaps reflecting the fact that a certain amount of 'roughness' and 'toughness' is considered to be a desirable masculine attribute in our society (see Trudgill, 1972: 183). Behaviour that is unacceptable for girls, in other words, is considered to be normal for boys. Six boys – Nobby, Rob, Benny, Tommy, Dave and Pete – were recorded in small groups with their teacher, for about twenty minutes each. Two other boys – Jeff and Derek – were recorded in a class discussion. Their teacher had not been able to record them in small groups since this apparently involved advance planning, which was not possible where children were irregular attenders. These recordings provide only a small amount of data compared to that obtained for the same speakers in spontaneous conversation at the playgrounds, but they do provide an adequate basis for comparing the use of some of the more frequently occurring linguistic features in vernacular style and in school style.

9.3 Variation in speech style

Table 50 shows the frequency with which nine nonstandard linguistic features occur in the vernacular style and in the school style of the eight boys for whom school recordings were available. The first five features are all used less often by the boys in their school style: nonstandard *was* occurs only slightly less often, but the other features show a marked decrease in frequency. Nonstandard *come* remains invariant in the boys' school style. Nonstandard *what* and *ain't*, on the other hand, do not decrease in frequency in school style; instead, they occur slightly more often.

At first glance, this seems a confusing state of affairs. The figures for the first five features in the Table suggest that the boys are susceptible to the overt norms of society, for when they are at school they use fewer

Table 50. *Stylistic variation in the frequency indices for nonstandard features*

Feature	Vernacular style	School style
Class A		
nonstandard *-s*	57.03	31.49
nonstandard *has*	46.43	35.71
nonstandard *was*	91.67	88.57
negative concord	90.70	66.67
Class B		
nonstandard *never*	49.21	15.38
nonstandard *what*	50.00	54.55
Class C		
nonstandard *come*	100.00	100.00
ain't = auxiliary HAVE	93.02	100.00
ain't = copula BE	74.47	77.78

nonstandard forms and more of the corresponding prestige standard English forms. The frequency of occurrence of the remaining features, on the other hand, suggests the reverse: in most cases there is a slight increase in frequency in school style.

This kind of group analysis, however, reveals more about the nature of sociolinguistic variables than it does about the behaviour of the speakers who use them. A Labovian analysis typically classifies linguistic variables into 'indicators' and 'markers' on the basis of their correlation with nonlinguistic features. Those variables that are correlated with social features of the context are indicators: a typical example is the Norwich variable (a:) (see Trudgill, 1974: 97–9), which, as Figure 6 shows, is correlated with the socioeconomic class of speakers. Socioeconomic class is perhaps the social feature that has been most commonly measured in sociolinguistic studies, but linguistic variables can also be indicators of the age, sex and ethnic group of speakers (see Labov, 1972b: 237), and, as we have seen in this study, of the degree to which speakers adhere to a vernacular sub-culture. Thus all the linguistic features in Table 50 are indicators: most are correlated with the sex of the speaker (only nonstandard *what*, in fact, is not) – though the correlation is clearest with negative concor, nonstandard *come* and *ain't*, as Table 37 shows. Nonstandard *-s*, *has*, *was*, *never* and *what* also show regular correlation with the boys' vernacular culture index, and since adherence to the vernacular culture

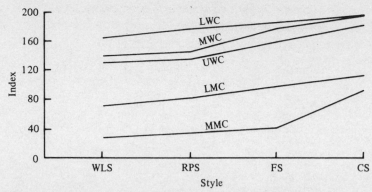

Figure 6   Variable (a:) by class and style (from Trudgill, 1974: 98)
LWC – Lower working class   WLS – Word list style
MWC – Middle working class   RPS – Reading passage
UWC – Upper working class   style
LMC – Lower middle class   FS   – Formal speech
MMC – Middle middle class   CS   – Casual speech

can be ordered hierarchically, these five features can be considered 'stratified indicators' (see Labov, 1972b: 237).

Markers are more highly developed sociolinguistic variables (Labov, 1972b: 237) that show not only social variation but also stylistic variation. Again, a typical example can be found in Trudgill's Norwich study: Figure 7 shows that Norwich (ng) is regularly correlated not only with the socioeconomic class of speakers but also with speech style. The (ng) index increases for all speakers, irrespective of their socioeconomic class, as speech style becomes less formal. The group figures in Table 50 allow

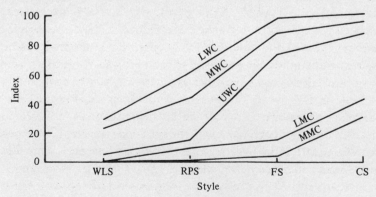

Figure 7   Variable (ng) by class and style (from Trudgill, 1974: 92)

us to identify those features of Reading English that appear to be markers: this includes the features in Class A, together with nonstandard *never* in Class B, which are all used less often by the boys in their school style than in their vernacular style. In order to confirm this classification it would be necessary to examine stylistic variation in the speech of the girls as well as the boys. Unfortunately, however, only one feature occurs with sufficient frequency in the girls' school recordings for a stylistic analysis to be attempted. Table 51 shows the frequency with which the seven girls recorded at school use the nonstandard suffix in their vernacular style and in their school style. As in the boys' speech, the nonstandard suffix occurs much less often in their school style. Sharon and Marlene are 'good' girls, however, who might be expected to use fewer nonstandard forms in school, so a more convincing confirmation of the status of the nonstandard suffix would be obtained if these two girls were not included in the analysis. Table 52, then, shows the frequency with which only Julie, Debbie, Mandy, Ann and Sue use the nonstandard suffix in their vernacular style and in their school style. Style-shifting still occurs, so the status of the nonstandard suffix as a sociolinguistic marker is confirmed.

Table 51. *Frequency indices for style-shifting in the girls' speech*

Feature	Vernacular style	School style
nonstandard -*s*	55.23	12.82

Table 52. *Frequency indices for style-shifting in the girls' speech (excluding Sharon and Marlene)*

Feature	Vernacular style	School style
nonstandard -*s*	66.25	50.00

Although this kind of classification is an essential component of sociolinguistic research (see Labov, 1972b: 243), the group analysis on which it rests may often need to be supplemented by other kinds of analyses in order to obtain a fuller understanding of the ways in which linguistic variation is related to social context. In order to understand the linguistic behaviour of individual peer group members – to analyse, that is, the extent to which they modify their speech to produce a style that they consider appropriate for school – it is necessary to compare the use of linguistic variables by individual speakers, rather than by groups of speakers. Unfortunately this is only possible here for present tense verb forms, for this is the only morphological feature that occurs in sufficient quantities for individual analyses to be performed. But this will provide at least some indication of the more subtle factors that are involved in sociolinguistic variation.

Table 53 shows the frequency of occurrence of nonstandard present tense verb forms in the speech of eight boys, in their vernacular style and in their school style. The boys are arranged in order of adherence to the vernacular culture: Nobby, Dave and Pete are Group 1 speakers, with a high vernacular culture index; Tommy, Jeff and Rob are Group 2 speakers, with a lower vernacular culture index; and Derek and Benny are Group 3 speakers, with the lowest vernacular culture index.

We can see from Table 53 that there are considerable differences in the ways in which individual speakers use the nonstandard suffix in their school style. Furthermore, these differences are completely unrelated to the degree to which speakers adhere to the vernacular culture: Nobby's use of nonstandard forms, for example, decreases by only 3.22 per cent in his school style, whilst the other Group 1 speakers – Dave and Pete – show a much sharper decrease. Jeff – a Group 2 speaker – uses no nonstandard forms at all in his school style, though his use of nonstandard forms in vernacular style is virtually the same as Rob's; and Rob and Tommy, who are also Group 2 speakers, continue to use nonstandard forms at school, though less often than they do at the playgrounds. Derek and Benny are Group 3 speakers: Derek, like Jeff, uses no nonstandard forms when he is at school; Benny, on the other hand, actually uses *more* nonstandard forms when he is at school than he does at the adventure playground.

Clearly, then, there is no simple correlation between the extent to which speakers are influenced by vernacular norms and the extent to which they change their use of nonstandard speech forms when they are at school. It is conceivable that some of the differences in individual behaviour are due to differences in the age of the boys: Nobby, for example, who continues to use a high proportion of nonstandard forms when he is at school, is only 11, so it is possible that he has not yet acquired the same ability to style-shift as the

Table 53. *Frequency indices for non-standard present tense verb forms*

Name	Vernacular style	School style
Group 1		
Nobby	81.00	77.78
Dave	70.83	34.62
Pete	71.43	54.55
Group 2		
Tommy	57.14	31.75
Jeff	45.00	0.00
Rob	45.71	33.33
Group 3		
Derek	38.46	0.00
Benny	31.58	54.17

other boys, who are aged between 13 and 16. We saw earlier, however, that there is no clear evidence from British studies as to the age at which style-shifting can be expected to begin. And in any case, an explanation in terms of age does not account for the extreme stylistic sensitivity shown by Jeff and Derek, who use no nonstandard present tense forms at school; nor does it account for the eccentric behaviour of Benny, who uses more nonstandard present tense forms when he is at school than when he is at the playground.

A closer examination of the situation in which the school recordings were made, however, can suggest some explanation for these individual differences in style-shifting.

Benny, for example, was recorded with Nobby and Rob by their form-master. The teacher had been asking the boys about their activities outside school, and they were telling him about a disco that they were building. This was a project that was very important to all three boys, though Rob was the chief organiser, and it was currently taking up a great deal of their spare time. The teacher was well meaning but was not familiar with the kind of recording equipment that the boys were using, and he was having to struggle hard to understand the conversation, as the extract below shows:

Rob:　　　　I helps my dad build a double deck.
Teacher:　　Pardon? You –

Rob:	Got a double deck, and I help me dad build it.
Teacher:	Double deck? Well, what's that exactly?
Rob:	Two decks.
	(silence)
Nobby:	Disco.
Rob:	Disco.
Teacher:	A disco?
Rob:	Mmm.
Teacher:	What, does your dad run a disco, then?
Rob:	No, I'm hoping to. To run one down Newtown School.
Nobby:	He's building it.
Teacher:	And he, he's building it, is he?
	[Nobby is referring to Rob, but the teacher assumes it is Rob's father who is building the disco.]
Rob:	Mmm.
Teacher:	And he's got records, and all the rest of it, has he?
Rob:	Oh, I got them, yeah.
Teacher:	Oh, I see. And what, he's going to play for, so that people can dance in the evenings. You're gonna hire Newtown School Hall, all that kind of thing, are you? And how far have you got with that, then?
Rob:	There's only another two speakers, in it?
Benny:	Yeah, something like that.
Teacher:	Pardon?
Nobby:	Two speakers to get now.
Teacher:	You've built it apart from the two speakers?
Rob:	Yeah.

However well intentioned the teacher and the boys may have felt towards each other at the beginning of this conversation, the immense differences that existed between them in terms of their interests and experience must have become increasingly apparent as the conversation went on. And in fact, Nobby and Benny would *not* necessarily have been well intentioned towards their teacher. Both these boys had said at the adventure playground that they hated school and their teachers, and they had made extremely derisory remarks about them. Benny was a chronic truant and had only just returned to school after an absence of a whole term, and Nobby attended school only intermittently. Rob, on the other hand, attended school regularly. He was very much in awe of his father – he had once quickly put out a cigarette when his father walked past the playground, as he was not allowed to smoke at home – and so he did not dare to stay away from school. This meant, of course, that he knew the teacher quite well, whereas the other boys did not, and it also meant that he had had more exposure than the other boys to the culture of the school.

This allows us to suggest an explanation for the different ways in which these three boys use nonstandard present tense forms when they are at school. We can assume that Rob, who attends school regularly, has come to accept that the school requires a specific kind of behaviour. He adapts his speech accordingly, using a higher proportion of the prestigious standard English verb forms than he does normally. Nobby and Benny, on the other hand, appear *not* to have accepted the cultural norms of the school – Benny more so than Nobby, since he stays away from school more often. The nonstandard present tense suffix is a sensitive marker of vernacular loyalty, as we have seen, and this means that it can be used to assert allegiance to the vernacular peer group culture rather than to the school. Thus Nobby uses virtually the same high frequency of nonstandard present tense forms when he is at school as when he is at the playground, making little or no concession to the social constraints of the school. Benny reacts still more strongly than Nobby. He is not closely involved in the peer group culture, and this is reflected in his vernacular speech by a relatively low frequency index for nonstandard present tense forms. But because the nonstandard suffix is a marker of vernacular loyalty, he is able to assert his independence and hostility when he is at school by using an *increased* proportion of nonstandard forms.

The linguistic behaviour of Dave, Pete and Tommy can also be explained by looking in more detail at the situation in which the school recording was made. They were recorded together by a teacher whom they knew well. He had taken a group of boys, including these three, on camping and fishing trips, so presumably they associated him not only with the school but also with their outside activities. The conversation was initially about one of these weekends; it moved on to racing cars and motorbikes, topics that were of interest to both the teacher and the boys, and then to the boys' leisure activities. An extract from this recording was given in Section 2.3; it provides a striking comparison with the extract from the school recording of Nobby, Rob and Benny. Dave, Pete and Tommy all use fewer nonstandard present tense forms when they are at school, with their teacher, than when they are at the adventure playground. They appear, in other words, to adapt their speech and to accept, to some extent, the constraints of the school.

This is interesting, since Dave and Pete, in particular, are strongly involved in the vernacular culture – they are Group 1 speakers, like

Nobby. Nobby, as we have seen, does not use a significantly lower proportion of nonstandard present tense forms when he is at school, and this suggests that here it is not so much the attitude of Dave, Pete and Tommy towards the *school* that influences their use of nonstandard forms as their attitude towards the *teacher*.

It has been shown that, other things being equal, when speakers are well disposed towards each other their accents tend to 'converge' – in other words, each speaker adapts his speech towards that of the other (see Giles and Smith, 1979; Thakerar, Giles and Cheshire, 1982). It is reasonable to assume that this process may extend to morphological and syntactic features as well as to phonological features – though the accommodation is likely to be a one-way process if one speaker normally uses nonstandard forms and the other does not. Thus the fact that Dave, Pete and Tommy have a good relationship with their teacher (based in part on shared experiences outside school) may account for the fact that these boys increase their use of standard English present tense forms in their school recording by a significant amount, whereas Nobby and Benny do not. Even Rob, who also uses an increased proportion of standard English forms when he is at school, shows a much smaller increase than Dave, Pete or Tommy.

The ways in which the boys adapt their speech style when they are at school, then, depend partly on the extent of their involvement with the school culture and partly on the nature of their relationship with the teacher. We must also assume, of course, that there are many other factors affecting speech style that we have not been able to take into account here. The state of mind of the speaker, to suggest just one example, would clearly affect speech style – if Dave had recently had an altercation with his teacher we might expect him to use a higher proportion of nonstandard present tense forms, since this would assert his temporary rejection of the school culture. It is worth noting, in this respect, that all the speakers considered so far continue to use *some* nonstandard present tense forms when they are at school. Even those boys who show a marked decrease in frequency still use the nonstandard suffix at least 30 per cent of the time, so they are still expressing some degree of allegiance to vernacular norms.

This is not the case, however, for Jeff and Derek. These boys use no nonstandard present tense forms in their school style, although they both use them fairly extensively in their vernacular style, as Table 53 shows. Again, it is helpful to consider the situations in which the school recordings were made, especially since both Jeff's and Derek's recordings took place under similar conditions. They were recorded on separate occasions, by different teachers; both the recordings, however, were of class discussions, where about twenty pupils and the teacher were present. The situation here, therefore, is different from those considered so far. Furthermore, on both occasions Jeff and Derek were the only peer group members in the class – whereas the other school recordings that were made featured the teacher and three boys who were members of the same peer group and who spent much of their time together when they were *not* at school.

Both Jeff and Derek took an active part in the class discussions, partly because they were deliberately encouraged to do so by their teachers and partly because the teacher had intentionally chosen topics on which they had strong views (football hooliganism, in Jeff's case, and truancy, in Derek's). The kind of discussion that took place can be seen from the following extract, which is taken from Derek's recording. The class had begun by discussing the merits of raising the school-leaving age; Derek was firmly against raising it, whilst Claudine, a West Indian girl, was in favour of raising it. Wayne was attempting to introduce some humour into the discussion.

Derek:	All right, Claudine, what have you learnt this week that you ain't learnt last week?
Wayne:	Yeah, that's a good one.
Claudine:	Well . . . in what lesson?
Derek:	Any lesson.
Claudine:	Any. Right. In typing, right. I learned about how to do indentation. And all this stuff that I hadn't done before. Right?
Derek:	What, this week?
Claudine:	Yeah, this week. I hadn't done it before.
Derek:	And you didn't do it last week?
Claudine:	No, I didn't.
Derek:	What else?
Claudine:	And commas. We're doing about, what is it –
Wayne:	Cabbages!
	(laughter)
Claudine:	Oh, shut up.
	(laughter)
Teacher:	Derek, what have you learnt this week that you didn't, well, you've only been here a day.
	(laughter)
Derek:	I've been here four days.

Teacher:	Have you? Did you learn anything at all this week that you didn't learn last week?
Derek:	No.
Teacher:	Not one thing?
Derek:	I weren't here any last week. (laughter)
Teacher:	You didn't learn anything this week that you didn't know about before?
Derek:	Well, I ain't learnt nothing. This week.
Wayne:	Nobody's taught him anything.
Derek:	I reckon I know enough, so that should be all right, really.
Teacher:	Enough for what?
Wayne:	He could read and write.
Derek:	To get meself a job.
Wayne:	He could read and write in the doss-house.
Derek:	A couple of years ago, years and years ago, as long as you could read and write, that was it.
Teacher:	And you reckon that was a good thing?
Derek:	Yeah. I reckon it's just as good as now.
Claudine:	But another thing, Derek, more employment, employers want, a high standard of, um –
Other pupil:	Brains.
Claudine:	Yeah.
Wayne:	Yeah, 'cos you don't really want to grow up to be a cabbage, do you?
Claudine:	Oh, shut up. They need you to have, um, more exams and everything before they'll give you a job, in't it?
Wayne:	Yeah. 'Cos you don't want to go into a job and end up like a cabbage.
Teacher:	What do you say to that?
Derek:	I didn't hear it.
Wayne:	Cabbages.
Teacher:	It's because of people, bleating. Claudine said that now jobs need more qualifications . . .
Claudine:	Some of them, you can start at the bottom and then you've got to pass some examination before you go up.
Derek:	Yeah, then that'd prove you'd done summat. For yourself.
Claudine:	But if you, say maths, you're no good at maths and they want you to do maths exams before you can go higher up, how will you get to that stage, now? You've got to stay at the bottom, haven't you?
Derek:	No. You could bloody study outside school.

Clearly Derek felt strongly about the views he was expressing, and it might be expected that he would therefore pay little attention to his speech, and use the same proportion of nonstandard speech forms as he does in his vernacular style. It might also be expected that since the views he was expressing conform to the norms of the vernacular culture (i.e. that school, as it stands, is a waste of time), he would assert his allegiance to this culture by using the nonstandard present tense suffix, which is a marker of vernacular loyalty. In fact, however, both Derek and Jeff used only standard English present tense forms in the class discussions. Possibly the fact that there were no other peer group members present meant that the boys were more susceptible to the pressures of the norms of the school culture. It is also possible that the *number* of speakers who are present has an extremely important effect on speech style (see O'Donnell and Todd, 1980: 78). It may not be appropriate, for example, to assert allegiance linguistically to the vernacular culture when speaking in front of twenty people with whom one is not on intimate terms and who are not themselves involved in the culture. The overall formality of the situation, in other words, may override Derek's option of displaying linguistically his allegiance to the vernacular culture.

There may also be other factors responsible for the fact that neither Derek nor Jeff used the nonstandard suffix in the school recordings. It is clear, though, that speech style cannot be explained by a simple analysis in terms of formality or informality, no matter how formality is defined. There is a large amount of personal variation in the response of individual speakers to different situations. Some responses may be completely idiosyncratic, and not open to formal analysis. Others may reflect social factors which affect all speakers. And, of course, proper conversations are interactional processes, in which speakers are continually reassessing the social context and adjusting their speech in order to produce an appropriate style. To analyse the speech style used during a speech event as if it were a constant quality, then, is to create a methodological abstraction which may be necessary but which must not be allowed to distort our understanding of the processes that are involved.

Furthermore, it seems that different linguistic features have different potentialities for stylistic variation. Not all variables enter into stylistic variation – we saw earlier that this is the basis for the distinction that is often drawn between indicators and markers. Use of the nonstandard present tense suffix, as we have seen, can assert the degree of allegiance to the vernacular culture that speakers feel is appropriate to the occasion. We may assume that other sociolinguistic markers can convey other kinds of social information.

We do not yet know very much about the stylistic resources of the language system. There seems little doubt, however, that speakers are able to exploit these resources in order to convey different kinds of information – in other words, that stylistic variation has a distinct social function.

Conclusion

The linguistic analysis that forms the main part of this study began by listing the morphological and syntactic differences between standard English and what was termed 'Reading English'. By this was meant the variety of English spoken by the adolescent peer groups who provided the data for the analysis. But the use of the term 'Reading English' may have been misleading, for it implies that this is a distinct variety that can be described in terms of its linguistic characteristics. As the analysis progressed it became clear that it would be extremely difficult to define 'Reading English', for almost all the nonstandard features that might be considered characteristic of the variety are variable features that alternate in occurrence with the corresponding standard English forms. This means that 'pure' Reading English does not exist other than as a theoretical abstraction.

A similar state of affairs, of course, exists for standard English. Standard English has never been rigorously defined (see Macaulay, 1977: 68–74), and variation is as characteristic of this variety as of any other. This is well illustrated by Quirk's analysis (1968) of relative clauses in spoken standard English, which isolates some linguistic constraints controlling variation in the forms of the relative pronoun. As yet, however, there is little or no empirical evidence concerning the nonlinguistic factors that control variation within standard English. But as far as *nonstandard* English is concerned, it seems that a continuum exists, with speakers using nonstandard features in response to a wide range of linguistic and nonlinguistic factors. Some of the nonlinguistic factors are beyond the control of the speaker in that they are ascribed social characteristics. For example, the proportion of nonstandard forms that are used is to some extent determined by age, sex and socioeconomic class. But speakers can also choose (possibly at a subconscious level) to use nonstandard features in such a way that they convey different kinds of social information, as was shown in Chapter 9.

A further question is raised by the fact that adolescents were used as informants. Working-class adolescent peer groups were chosen as subjects on the grounds that they would use a large number of nonstandard forms, which was necessary for the analysis of variation. It is possible, however, that their use of language is not typical, for they may conform to social norms that will be outgrown as they leave adolescence. This is particularly true of vocabulary items, and may, therefore, apply to the 'vernacular' verbs discussed in Section 4.1.7. All the morphological and syntactic variables analysed in this study, however, were overheard in the speech of adults in Reading, and some of the linguistic constraints that control variation in the speech of the adolescents also control the speech of elderly speakers, though to a lesser extent. It seems reasonable to conclude that although the nature and strength of the linguistic and social constraints governing variation *may* be specific to the English used by adolescents, the principles that are involved are general ones: variation is often associated with language change, for example, and it can fulfil an important social function.

It is worth stressing that the linguistic differences between standard English and the nonstandard variety (or 'continuum') that is spoken in Reading are marginal in nature. The varieties have a very large 'common core' (see Quirk et al., 1972: 13–14), and the morphological and syntactic features that have been discussed in this study are linguistically relatively trivial. Many of the features illustrate a tendency towards a simpler, more regular system in the nonstandard variety: the use of the third person reflexive pronoun *hisself* is an example of this, as are the nonstandard verbal paradigms. There is a tendency towards the elimination of redundant elements, which also leads to a more regular system: thus subject marking in the verb form is eliminated by the use of nonstandard *was* and by the use of the nonstandard present tense suffix, the plural marker is lost in nouns of measurement, and there is no formal distinction between some adjectives and adverbs. Some nonstandard features, on the other hand, allow formal methods of stylistic emphasis that do not exist in standard English. Thus both negative concord and nonstandard *never* emphasise negation in a sentence; the 'double-comparison' of some adverbs emphasises their comparative function; and the use of the 'conditional' tense in both clauses of a sentence emphasises the conditional element.

None of the nonstandard features is peculiar to Reading English. Some features, such as negative concord and *ain't*, occur in most, if not all,

British and American nonstandard varieties. Others are more localised – the nonstandard present tense suffix, for example, occurs in parts of the North of England, and particularly in the Southwest and in South Wales (Hughes and Trudgill, 1979).

There are several possible approaches to the analysis of variation in language; scaling, for example, has sometimes proved to be useful (see Bailey, 1973). But a quantitative approach has the advantage that it can uncover a wide range of linguistic and social factors that control variation. It has been found, for example, that the use of some nonstandard features is subject to strong linguistic constraints. Occurrence of the nonstandard present tense forms of HAVE and DO depends on whether the verb is an auxiliary verb or a full verb; and the occurrence of other nonstandard present tense verb forms depends on the nature of a following complement. The discovery that these constraints exist has implications for both synchronic and diachronic linguistic theory. Synchronically, the fact that auxiliary HAVE behaves differently in the nonstandard variety from full verb HAVE supports the analysis of auxiliaries as a category that is distinct from full verbs; and the fact that HAVE, when followed by a *to-* infinitive, behaves in the same way as the full verb supports its analysis as a full verb (see Section 4.1.1). Analysis of the use of nonstandard *never* by the peer groups is also able to resolve problems concerning the syntactic status of the form (see Cheshire, 1981b). Thus empirical studies of language use have an important part to play in the synchronic analysis of language structure.

The existence of linguistic constraints on variation also has important implications for diachronic linguistics. It is known that sound changes begin in a specific phonetic environment, affecting at first only a small number of words, and that they gradually spread through the lexicon (see Chen and Hsieh, 1971; Chen and Wang, 1975). This study has suggested that morphological/syntactic change proceeds in precisely the same way. For example, the nonstandard present tense suffix, which at one time occurred categorically throughout the present tense paradigm of regular verbs, appears first to have been lost in a specific syntactic environment – that of a following tense marked complement. There are indications that this change is spreading from one syntactic environment to another, in a series of overlapping movements, in just the same way that sound change spreads through the lexicon: thus in the peer groups' speech the change is almost completed in the environment of a following tense marked complement, and it is also under way in a different environment – that of a following complement where tense is *not* marked. Similarly, the use of *in't* rather than *ain't* appears to be beginning in a specific syntactic environment – that of tag questions. Furthermore, it seems likely that syntactic environment is a crucial factor in the development of this kind of change. The same syntactic environment can 'host' more than one morphological/syntactic change: a following tense marked complement, for example, is conducive not only to the loss of the present tense suffix but also to the loss of *never* as a negative preterite form.

The extent to which speakers use nonstandard features is dependent not only on the linguistic context in which they occur but also on a number of sociolinguistic factors. The sociolinguistic analysis of variation, in Part III of this study, focused on two levels of analysis. Firstly, an analysis of the use of nonstandard features by different *groups* of speakers appeared to confirm the Labovian classification of sociolinguistic variables into indicators and markers, and showed, in addition, that different variables have different kinds of social significance. For the boys, the nonstandard present tense suffix, nonstandard *has*, *was*, and *never*, and negative concord all act as symbols of adherence to the vernacular culture; some, but not all, of these features act in a similar way for the girls. The nonstandard past tense form *come* is particularly interesting, since it is an invariant feature for boys, with no clear social function, whilst for girls it is a symbol of vernacular loyalty. Conversely, nonstandard *has* and *never* are symbols of vernacular loyalty for boys, but not for girls. Thus not only are the nonstandard features used with different frequencies by male and female speakers (as has been amply demonstrated in previous studies), but they may also have different social significances.

A subsequent analysis in terms of the use of nonstandard features by *individual* speakers showed how speakers are able to exploit these sociolinguistic resources of the language system. The fact that speakers use language to symbolise personal identity is, of course, well known (see, for example, Le Page, 1968: 192); this study, however, has been able to point to the kinds of factors that may influence the *degree* to which speakers exploit these linguistic resources. Several different factors, for example, affect the extent to which speakers choose to identify with the vernacular culture: these include the relationship between the speaker and the other people present, and the speaker's attitude to the situation.

There were no data available for an analysis of the ways in which features with the social function of sex markers are used by individual speakers on different occasions. It is logical to suppose, however, that this function may be exploited in just the same way – that speakers may be able to use variation to assert different degrees of 'femininity' or 'masculinity' in the same way that they can assert loyalty to the vernacular culture.

The analysis of the individual's use of nonstandard features in different social contexts leads us to question the validity of the Labovian concept of style, which sees the proportion of nonstandard features that are used as directly linked to the amount of attention that speakers give to their speech. It has been suggested in this study that this is over-simplistic, since in some cases paying attention to speech appears to result in the use of an *increased* number of nonstandard forms. A more realistic approach to style is to view it as the individual's linguistic response to the social occasion. This takes into account the fact that different speakers may react in different ways, for a number of reasons, to what may appear objectively to be the same situation. This is not to deny that there may be some general characteristics of social occasions that can override more personal reactions to produce a definitive 'formal' situation. We saw in Chapter 9 that speaking in front of a large number of 'outsiders' may be an example of this. But the effect that overall formality has on speech depends on the sociolinguistic status and the social function of the different linguistic variables. The nonstandard present tense suffix appears to be extremely sensitive to overall formality. We can imagine, however, that the boys' use of nonstandard *come*, which remained invariant for all boys in both speech styles, might be entirely insensitive to formality.

A great deal remains to be discovered about the nature and function of variation in language. The aim of this study has been to make some contribution towards our understanding.

Appendix

Frequency indices for realisations of ain't *(full versions of Tables 26 and 27)*

| | 3rd singular subjects | | | | | |
	Declarative sentences			Tag questions		
Auxiliary HAVE	*ain't*	*in't*	*hasn't*	*ain't*	*in't*	*hasn't*
Orts Road boys	100.00	0.00	0.00	14.29	85.71	0.00
Shinfield boys	(100.00)	(0.00)	(0.00)	–	–	–
Shinfield girls	60.00	0.00	40.00	(100.00)	(0.00)	(0.00)
All speakers	82.35	0.00	17.65	33.33	66.67	0.00
Copula BE	*ain't*	*in't*	*isn't*	*ain't*	*in't*	*isn't*
Orts Road boys	62.50	7.50	30.00	0.00	100.00	0.00
Shinfield boys	83.33	0.00	16.67	(25.00)	(75.00)	(0.00)
Shinfield girls	40.00	5.71	54.29	3.85	84.62	11.54
All speakers	54.32	6.17	39.51	2.86	92.86	4.29
Auxiliary BE	*ain't*	*in't*	*isn't*	*ain't*	*in't*	*isn't*
Orts Road boys	80.00	0.00	20.00	(0.00)	(100.00)	(0.00)
Shinfield boys	(50.00)	(0.00)	(50.00)	(0.00)	(66.67)	(33.33)
Shinfield girls	20.00	20.00	60.00	–	–	–
All speakers	50.00	8.33	41.67	0.00	85.71	14.29

| | Non-3rd singular subjects | | | | | |
	Declarative sentences			Tag questions		
Auxiliary HAVE	*ain't*	*in't*	*haven't*	*ain't*	*in't*	*haven't*
Orts Road boys	82.86	0.00	17.14	57.14	42.86	0.00
Shinfield boys	(100.00)	(0.00)	(0.00)	(100.00)	(0.00)	(0.00)
Shinfield girls	64.00	0.00	36.00	(66.67)	(0.00)	(33.33)
All speakers	76.56	0.00	23.44	72.73	27.27	0.00
Copula BE	*ain't*	*in't*	*aren't*	*ain't*	*in't*	*aren't*
Orts Road boys	60.00	0.00	40.00	16.67	83.33	0.00
Shinfield boys	100.00	0.00	0.00	(100.00)	(0.00)	(0.00)
Shinfield girls	42.11	0.00	57.89	(50.00)	(50.00)	0.00
All speakers	58.33	0.00	41.67	40.00	60.00	0.00

Auxiliary BE	ain't	in't	aren't	ain't	in't	aren't
Orts Road boys	76.00	0.00	24.00	42.86	57.14	0.00
Shinfield boys	61.54	0.00	38.46	(100.00)	(0.00)	(0.00)
Shinfield girls	27.27	0.00	72.73	(0.00)	(0.00)	(0.00)
All speakers	61.22	0.00	38.78	44.44	55.56	0.00

Bibliography

Abrams, M. 1959. *The Teenage Consumer*. London: London Press Exchange.

Allcorn, D. H. 1955. 'The social development of young men in an English industrial suburb'. Ph.D. thesis, University of Manchester.

Andry, R. G. 1960. *Delinquency and Parental Pathology*. London: Methuen.

Bailey, C.-J. N. 1973. *Variation and Linguistic Theory*. Arlington, Va.: Center for Applied Linguistics.

Barnes, W. 1886. *A Glossary of the Dorset Dialect with a Grammar*. London: Trübner. Reprinted 1970, Guernsey: Stevens-Cox (The Toucan Press).

Bhatnager, J. 1970. *Immigrants at School*. London: Cornmarket Press.

Brown, K. and Millar, B. 1978. 'Auxiliary verbs in Edinburgh speech'. Work in Progress II. Department of Linguistics, University of Edinburgh.

Chambers, J. K. and Trudgill, P. 1980. *Dialectology*. Cambridge: Cambridge University Press.

Chen, M. and Hsieh, H.-I. 1971. 'The time variable in phonological change'. *Journal of Linguistics*, 7, pp. 1–14.

Chen, M. and Wang, W. S.-Y. 1975. 'Sound change: actuation and implementation'. *Language*, 51, 2, pp. 255–81.

Cheshire, J. 1978. 'Present tense verbs in Reading English'. In *Sociolinguistic Patterns in British English*, ed. P. Trudgill, pp. 52–68. London: Edward Arnold.

1981a. 'Variation in the use of *ain't* in an urban British English dialect'. *Language in Society*, 10, 3, pp. 365–81.

1981b. 'British nonstandard *never* and the problem of where grammars stop'. MS.

Clarke, J. 1973. 'The skinheads and the study of youth culture'. Occasional Paper. Birmingham: Centre for Contemporary Cultural Studies.

Classification of Occupations, 1971. Office of Population Censuses and Surveys. London: H.M.S.O.

Cohen, A. K. 1955. *Delinquent Boys*. New York: The Free Press.

Cohen, P. 1976. 'Subcultural conflict and working-class community'. In *The Process of Schooling*, ed. M. Hammersley and P. Woods, pp. 41–7. London and Henley: Routledge and Kegan Paul in association with the Open University Press.

Downes, D. 1966. *The Delinquent Solution*. London: Routledge and Kegan Paul.

1970. 'Peer groups'. In *The Sociology of Modern Britain*, ed. E. Butterworth and D. Weir, pp. 149–54. London: William Collins (Fontana).

Fillmore, C. 1966. 'On the syntax of preverbs'. Unpublished paper, Ohio State University.

Finch, F. H. and Hoehn, A. J. 1951. 'Measuring socio-economic or cultural status: a comparison of methods'. *Journal of Social Psychology*, 33, pp. 51–67.

Giles, H. and St Clair, R. (eds.) 1979. *Language and Social Psychology*. Oxford: Blackwell.

Giles, H. and Smith, P. 1979. 'Accommodation theory: optional levels of convergence'. In *Language and Social Psychology*, ed. H. Giles and R. St Clair, pp. 45–65. Oxford: Blackwell.

Hebdige, D. 1979. *Subculture: the meaning of style*. London: Methuen.

Henry, J. 1963. *Culture against Man*. New York: Random House (Penguin edition, 1973).

Hewett, S. 1892. *The Peasant Speech of Devon*. London: Elliot Stock.

Huddleston, R. 1969. 'Some observations on tense and deixis in English'. *Language*, 45, 4, pp. 777–806.

Hudson, R. A. 1975. 'The meaning of questions'. *Language*, 51, 1, pp. 1–31.

Hughes, G. A. and Trudgill, P. 1979. *English Accents and Dialects: an introduction to regional and social varieties of British English*. London: Edward Arnold.

Hymes, D. 1967. 'Models of the interaction of language and social setting'. *Journal of Social Issues*, 23, 2, pp. 8–28.

Jespersen, O. 1940. *A Modern English Grammar on Historical Principles*. Part v. Copenhagen: Ejnar Munksgaard.

Klima, E. 1964. 'Negation in English'. In *The Structure of Language: readings in the philosophy of language*, ed. J. A. Fodor and J. J. Katz, pp. 246–323. Englewood Cliffs, N.J.: Prentice-Hall.

Kruisinga, E. and Erades, P. A. 1953. *An English Grammar*. Vol. 1. Groningen: Nordhoff.

Labov, W. 1965. 'Stages in the acquisition of standard English'. In *Social Dialects and Language Learning*, ed. R. Shuy, pp. 77–103. Champaign, Ill.: National Council of Teachers of English.

  1966. *The Social Stratification of English in New York City*. Washington, D.C.: Center for Applied Linguistics.

  1970. 'The study of language in its social context'. *Studium Generale*, 23, 1, pp. 30–87.

  1972a. *Language in the Inner City*. Philadelphia: University of Pennsylvania Press.

  1972b. *Sociolinguistic Patterns*. Philadelphia: University of Pennsylvania Press.

  1972c. 'Some principles of linguistic methodology'. *Language in Society*, 1, 1, pp. 97–120.

  1972d. 'Negative attraction and negative concord in English grammar'. *Language*, 48, 4, pp. 773–818.

  1973a. 'Where do grammars stop?' In *Sociolinguistics: current trends and prospects*, ed. R. Shuy, pp. 43–88. Washington, D.C.: Georgetown University Press.

1973b. 'The linguistic consequences of being a lame'. In *Language in Society*, 2, 1, pp. 81–115. Also in W. Labov, *Language in the Inner City*, 1972, pp. 255–92. Philadelphia: University of Pennsylvania Press.

Labov, W., Cohen, P., Robins, C. and Lewis, J. 1968. *A Study of the Non-standard English of Negro and Puerto Rican Speakers in New York City.* Vols. I and II. Final Report, Co-operative Research Project 3288. Washington, D.C.: U.S. Office of Health, Education and Welfare.

Le Page, R. B. 1968. 'Problems of description in multilingual communities'. *Transactions of the Philological Society*, pp. 189–212.

Macaulay, R. K. S. 1977. *Language, Social Class and Education.* Edinburgh: Edinburgh University Press.

McRobbie, A. and Garber, J. 1976. 'Girls and subcultures'. In *Resistance through Rituals*, ed. S. Hall and T. Jefferson, pp. 209–22. London: Hutchinson.

Maxim, J. Forthcoming. 'A grammatical analysis of language in the elderly'. Ph.D. thesis, University of Reading.

Mays, J. B. 1954. *Growing Up in the City.* Liverpool: Liverpool University Press.

Miller, W. B. 1958. 'Lower class culture as a generating milieu of gang delinquency'. *Journal of Social Issues*, 14, 3, pp. 5–19.

Milroy, L. 1980. *Language and Social Networks.* Oxford: Blackwell.

Moss, M. H. 1973. *Deprivation and Disadvantage?* Open University Course Book E262:8. Bletchley, Bucks.: Open University Press.

O'Donnell, W. R. and Todd, L. 1980. *Variety in Contemporary English.* London: George Allen and Unwin.

Orton, H. and Dieth, E. 1962–71. *Survey of English Dialects.* Published for the University of Leeds: E. J. Arnold.

Orton, H., Sanderson, S. and Widdowson, J. (eds.) 1978. *The Linguistic Atlas of England.* London: Croom Helm.

Palmer, F. R. 1965. *A Linguistic Study of the English Verb.* London: Longman.
 1974. *The English Verb.* London: Longman. (Revised version of F. R. Palmer, *A Linguistic Study of the English Verb*, 1965. London: Longman.)
 1979. 'Why auxiliaries are not main verbs'. *Lingua*, 47, pp. 1–25.

Pelto, P. J. 1970. *Anthropological Research: the structure of inquiry.* New York: Harper and Row.

Petyt, K. M. 1977. '"Dialect" and "accent" in the Industrial West Riding: a study of the changing speech of an urban area'. Ph.D. thesis, University of Reading.

Plowden Report. 1967. *Children and their Primary Schools.* A Report of the Central Advisory Council for Education (England). Vol. I: *The Report.* London: H.M.S.O.

Policansky, L. 1980. 'Verb concord variation in Belfast vernacular'. Paper presented to the Sociolinguistics Symposium, Walsall, West Midlands.

Quirk, R. 1968. 'Relative clauses in educated spoken English'. In R. Quirk, *Essays on the English Language Medieval and Modern*, pp. 94–108. London: Longman.

Quirk, R., Greenbaum, S., Leech, G. and Svartvik, J. 1972. *A Grammar of Contemporary English.* London: Longman.

Reid, E. 1978. 'Social and stylistic variation in the speech of children: some evidence from Edinburgh'. In *Sociolinguistic Patterns in British English*, ed. P. Trudgill, pp. 158–71. London: Edward Arnold.

Reid, I. 1977. *Social Class Differences in Britain*. London: Open Books.

Romaine, S. 1975. 'Linguistic variability in the speech of some Edinburgh schoolchildren'. M. Litt. thesis, University of Edinburgh.

1980. 'A critical overview of the methodology of urban British sociolinguistics'. *English World-Wide*, 1, 2, pp. 163–98.

(ed.) Forthcoming. *Sociolinguistic Patterns in Speech Communities*. London: Edward Arnold.

Rosen, H. 1972. *Language and Class: a critical look at the theories of Basil Bernstein*. Bristol: Falling Wall Press.

Smith, L. 1978. 'Sexist assumptions and female delinquency'. In *Women, Sexuality and Social Control*, ed. C. Smart and B. Smart, pp. 74–88. London: Routledge and Kegan Paul.

Stevens, M. 1954. 'The derivation of *ain't*'. *American Speech*, 29, pp. 196–201.

Strang, B. M. H. 1970. *A History of English*. London: Methuen.

Thakerar, J. N., Giles, H. and Cheshire, J. 1982. 'Psychological and linguistic parameters of speech accommodation theory'. In *Advances in the Social Psychology of Language*, ed. C. Fraser and K. R. Scherer. Cambridge: Cambridge University Press.

Trudgill, P. 1972. 'Sex, covert prestige and linguistic change in the urban British English of Norwich'. *Language in Society*, 1, 1, pp. 179–95.

1974. *The Social Differentiation of English in Norwich*. Cambridge: Cambridge University Press.

1975. *Accent, Dialect and the School*. London: Edward Arnold.

(ed.) 1978. *Sociolinguistic Patterns in British English*. London: Edward Arnold.

Wakelin, M. F. 1972. *English Dialects: an introduction*. London: Athlone Press.

Willis, P. 1976. 'The class significance of school counter-culture'. In *The Process of Schooling*, ed. M. Hammersley and P. Woods, pp. 188–200. London and Henley: Routledge and Kegan Paul in association with the Open University Press.

Willmott, P. 1966. *Adolescent Boys of East London*. London: Routledge and Kegan Paul.

Wilson, J. Forthcoming. 'Conversational strategies in adolescent encounters'. Ph.D. thesis, Queen's University, Belfast.

Wolfram, W. 1969. *A Sociolinguistic Description of Detroit Negro Speech*. Washington, D.C.: Center for Applied Linguistics.

1973. *Sociolinguistic Aspects of Assimilation: Puerto Rican English in New York City*. Arlington, Va.: Center for Applied Linguistics.

Wolfram, W. and Fasold, R. W. 1974. *The Study of Social Dialects in American English*. Englewood Cliffs, N.J.: Prentice-Hall.

Wolfson, N. 1976. 'Speech events and natural speech: some implications for sociolinguistic methodology'. *Language in Society*, 5, 2, pp. 189–209.

Index of authors

Abrams, M. 95
Andry, R. G. 96

Bailey, C.-J. N. 129
Barnes, W. 33
Bhatnager, J. 97
Brown, K. 57

Chambers, J. K. 11
Chen, M. 129
Cheshire, J. 53, 66, 85, 122, 129
Clarke, J. 97
Cohen, A. K. 96
Cohen, P. 12, 101

Dieth, E. 11, 46
Downes, D. 91, 92, 96

Erades, P. A. 65

Fasold, R. W. 51, 78
Finch, F. H. 97

Garber, J. 107
Giles, H. 5, 85, 112, 122
Greenbaum, S. 52, 65, 71, 128

Hebdige, D. 101
Henry, J. 107
Hewett, S. 33, 37
Hoehn, A. J. 97
Hsieh, H.-I. 129
Huddleston, R. 33
Hudson, R. A. 57, 58, 60–1
Hughes, G. A. 37, 44, 48, 52, 129
Hymes, D. 5

Jespersen, O. 53–4

Klima, E. 66
Kruisinga, E. 65

Labov, W. 6–7, 8–9, 10, 12, 27, 28, 60,
63–4, 65, 66, 67, 70, 85, 87, 89, 90–2,
94–5, 97–8, 112, 115–16, 117, 130, 131
Leech, G. 52, 65, 71, 128
Le Page, R. B. 85, 130
Lewis, J. 12

Macaulay, R. K. S. 9, 127
McRobbie, A. 107
Maxim, J. 11–12, 33–4, 37–9, 41–2, 61–2, 70
Mays, J. B. 91, 96
Millar, B. 57
Miller, W. B. 97
Milroy, L. 7, 111
Moss, M. H. 113

O'Donnell, W. R. 125
Orton, H. 11, 46, 54, 70

Palmer, F. R. 33, 35, 65
Pelto, P. J. 102
Petyt, K. M. 50
Policansky, L. 105

Quirk, R. 52, 65, 71, 73–4, 127, 128

Reid, E. 9
Reid, I. 21
Robins, C. 12
Romaine, S. 9, 12, 85
Rosen, H. 2

St Clair, R. 5
Sanderson, S. 54, 70
Smith, L. 96
Smith, P. 112, 122
Stevens, M. 53–4
Strang, B. M. H. 31
Svartvik, J. 52, 65, 71, 128

Thakerar, J. N. 85, 122
Todd, L. 125
Trudgill, P. 5–6, 11, 12, 28, 37, 44, 48,
52, 85, 87, 95, 114, 115–16, 129

Wakelin, M. F. 31
Wang, W. S.-Y. 129
Widdowson, J. 54, 70
Willis, P. 97

Willmott, P. 91
Wilson, J. 7
Wolfram, W. 51, 65, 78, 87
Wolfson, N. 112

General index

adjectives, interrogative 75
adolescent culture *see* teenage culture
adventure playgrounds, descriptions of:
  Orts Road 13; Shinfield 14
adverbs: comparative 80–1, 128; negative
  65, 70–1; non-distinction of adverbial
  and adjectival forms 80–1, 128
ages of speakers 22–3
ain't 51–63, 128–30; derivation of 53–4;
  phonetic realisations of 54–7; social
  variation in use of 104–6, 108–11;
  stylistic variation in use of 114–15
American English: *ain't* in 51, 128–9;
  conditional sentences in 50;
  demonstratives in 78; negative concord
  in 63, 128–9
analysis: of group speech 27–8, 85–111,
  114–17, 130; of individual speech 27–8,
  85, 118–25, 130; methods of 26–8; *see
  also* indices
any and *any-* compounds 63–7; *see also*
  negative concord
'apparent time' 11, 12; *see also* elderly
  speakers
auxiliaries, syntactic status of 33–4, 36–9,
  129

BE: negative present tense forms of *see
  ain't*; past tense forms of 44–6, 128,
  social variation in use of 104–6, 108–11,
  130, stylistic variation in use of 114–15
Black English Vernacular: *ain't* in 51;
  negative concord in 60, 63–4, 66; social
  variation in 90

class, socioeconomic *see* socioeconomic
  class
Classification of Occupations 24
come, as past tense form 48–9; social
  variation in use of 104–6, 108–11, 130;
  stylistic variation in use of 114–15
complements, as linguistic constraint on
  variation 39–43, 69–70, 129–30

conditional sentences, tense in 49–50,
  128
criminal activities 96–7, 98–9, 102–3, 106

data: collection of 5–15; nature of 15–20;
  see also recording procedures
demonstratives 78–9
diachronic syntax 42, 129; *see also*
  language change
DO: past tense forms of 37, 48–9; present
  tense forms of 34–9, 129, social
  variation in use of 104–6
'double-comparison' 80, 128

either 66–7
elderly speakers: linguistic constraints on
  speech of 128; recordings of 11–12; use
  of negative present tense forms of BE
  and HAVE 61–2; use of *never* 70; use
  of present tense forms of DO 37–9; use
  of present tense forms of HAVE 33–4;
  use of present tense forms of regular
  verbs 41–2
emphasis, in nonstandard English 128; by
  negative concord 63, 66–7; by *never*
  68, 71
ever 66

fieldwork methods *see* data
fighting 18–19, 92, 96, 106; skill at 88–9,
  98–9, 102–3
force marker (*in't*) 57–61, 63
formality, as sociolinguistic variable 6–7,
  112–25, 131
frequency index 27–8

Guttman scale 101–2

hardly 64–5
HAVE, present tense forms of 31–4;
  social variation in use of 104, 108–9,
  129–30; stylistic variation in use of
  114–15; *see also ain't*

housing: as indicator of socioeconomic class 21; of speakers 13, 14, 21
hypercorrection 37, 81

indices: frequency 27–8; multiple-item 97; vernacular culture 97–103, 115–17, linguistic indicators and markers of adherence to 102–6, 108–11, 121, 125, 130–1
indicators: Labovian 115–16; of adherence to vernacular culture 102–6, 108–11, 121, 125, 130–1; of socioeconomic class 21, 24
informants, choice of: adolescent 8–11, 13–14, 128; elderly 11–12
in't: as development from *ain't* 61–3, 130; as force marker 57–61, 63; as negative present tense form of BE and HAVE 54–7
interrogative adjectives 75
interrogative pronouns 75
'intrusive' *-s* 81
irregular verbs *see ain't*, BE, *come*, DO, HAVE, SEE

jobs 99–103
jokes 15–16

Labovian framework of analysis 6–7, 27, 115–17, 130–1
language change 10–11; in forms of *ain't* 53–4, 61–3, 130; in forms of DO 36–9; in forms of HAVE 33–4; in forms of *never* 70, 130; in present tense forms of regular verbs 41–2, 129–30
lexical constraints on variation: on forms of relative pronouns 74–5; on present tense forms of regular verbs 42–3
Linguistic Atlas of England, The 54, 70
linguistic backgrounds of speakers 23–4
linguistic constraints on variation 127–30; on *ain't* 52–3; on forms of relative pronouns 74–5; on negative past tense forms of BE 45–6; on *never* 69–70; on present tense forms of DO 35–6; on present tense forms of HAVE 32–3; on present tense forms of regular verbs 39–43
long-term participant-observation 8–9

markers: Labovian 115–17; sex 85–7, 108–11, 127, 130–1; of adherence to vernacular culture 102–6, 108–11, 121, 125, 130–1

measurement, nouns of 79–80, 128
multiple-item index 97

narratives 16–18, 20
negation, as linguistic constraint on variation 36, 45–6; *see also ain't*, emphasis in nonstandard English, negative concord, *never*
negative concord 63–7, 128–9; social variation in use of 108–11, 130; stylistic variation in use of 114–15
neither 66–7
never 67–71, 128, 129, 130; social variation in use of 104–5, 108–9; stylistic variation in use of 114–15; syntactic status of 66–7, 70–1
no and *no-* compounds 63–7; *see also* negative concord
norms: covert 12, 95; group 9, 10, 85, 118; overt 12, 95, 110, 114, 121; *see also* vernacular culture
nouns of measurement 79–80, 128

Observer's Paradox 7
occupation: as indicator of socioeconomic class 21, 24; of parents 24–5

past tense verb forms 44–50; *see also* BE, *come*, DO, SEE
phonological variation 1
peer groups: status in, as sociolinguistic variable 87–94; structure of 87–94
Plowden Report 13
prepositions 76–8
present tense forms of regular verbs 31–2, 39–43, 128–30; social variation in use of 104, 108–11; stylistic variation in use of 114–21
pronouns: interrogative 75; relative *see* relative pronouns; reflexive 79, 128

recording procedures: at adventure playgrounds 14–15, 18–19, 21; for elderly speakers 11–12; at school 15, 19–20, 113–14, 119–25
regular verbs *see* present tense forms of regular verbs
relative pronouns 72–5; social variation in use of 104–5, 108–9; stylistic variation in use of 114–15
reflexive pronouns 79, 128

-s: 'intrusive' 81; omission of, as marker of plurality 79–80, 128; as present tense suffix *see* present tense forms of regular verbs

school: attitudes of peer group members to 113–25, *see also* truancy; recordings at 15, 19–20, 113–14, 119–25; speech 19–20, 113–25

SEE, past tense forms of 47–9

sentence modifiers 66–7

sex: as sociolinguistic variable 85–7, 108–11, 127, 130–1; differences in peer group culture 106–7; differences in peer group structure 87–94; effect of on teachers' attitudes towards pupils 113–14

social networks 7

social variation 5–7, 12, 85–111; *see also* peer groups, sex, vernacular culture

socioeconomic class: as sociolinguistic variable 1–2, 5–7, 127; indicators of 21, 24

speech accommodation theory *see* speech convergence

speech convergence 112, 122

standard English features: as variable forms 1, 127; prestige of 12; relationship with socioeconomic class 12

style, of dress 9, 10, 100–3

style-shifting 8–9, 22, 117–19

Survey of English Dialects 11, 46

swearing 18–19, 101–3

syntactic splits 60

syntactic status: of auxiliaries 33–4, 36–9, 129; of *ever* 66; of *hardly* 65; of *never* 66–7, 70–1

tag questions: as linguistic constraint on variation 52–3, 55–7, 61–2; semantic functions of 57–61

teenage culture: 'legitimate' 95–7, 106–7; vernacular 94–103, 106–7, 121, 125, 130–1

tense, in conditional sentences 49–50, 128

truancy 10, 13, 96, 113, 120–1, 123

unsystematic observation 10

verb forms: past tense 44–50, *see also* BE, *come*, DO, SEE; present tense 31–43, *see also ain't*, conditional sentences, DO, HAVE, present tense forms of regular verbs; vernacular 42–3, 128

vernacular: culture 94–103, 106–7, 121, 125, 130–1, index *see* indices, *see also* indicators, markers; speech style 6–7, 12, 113–25; verbs 42–3, 128

weapons, carrying of 98–9, 102–3

what see relative pronouns